INVISIBLE
LINES *of*
CONNECTION

INVISIBLE
LINES *of*
CONNECTION
Sacred Stories
of the Ordinary

LAWRENCE KUSHNER

For People of All Faiths, All Backgrounds
JEWISH LIGHTS PUBLISHING · WOODSTOCK, VERMONT

Library of Congress Cataloging-in-Publication Data

Kushner, Lawrence, 1943—

    Invisible lines of connection : sacred stories of the ordinary /
Lawrence Kushner.
       p.   cm.
    ISBN 1-879045-52-4
    1. Spiritual biography—United States. 2. Parables. I. Title.
BM530.K87 1996
158.—dc20

10 9 8 7 6 5 4 3 2 1

Manufactured in the United States of America

Book and jacket designed and illustrated by the author

Published by Jewish Lights Publishing
A Division of LongHill Partners, Inc.
P.O. Box 237
Sunset Farm Offices—Route 4
Woodstock, Vermont 05091
Tel: (802) 457-4000
Fax: (802) 457-4004

for
Louis and Eleanor Skydell

"*I'll believe computers can think when you ask one a question and it replies, 'That reminds me of a story.'*"

—Gregory Bateson

"*The first premise of faith is to believe that there is no such thing as happenstance. . . .Every detail, small or great, they are all from the Holy One.*"

—Zaddok Hakohen of Lublin

STORIES

3. Responsibility

4. Connection

Stamp Collecting
(An Introduction)

My Uncle Art, a big, hairy barrel of a man who died almost thirty years ago, collected stamps. He had books and books filled with them. He kept them in a special room in his basement. Once he showed me his most valuable stamp. It was a misprint. Only a few thousand were accidentally released. It had a red border that said "U.S. Postage 24¢." Printed in blue in the center was an airplane, but the airplane was upside down! He said, "Sometimes what other people think is a mistake turns out to be valuable, so keep your eye out for airplanes that are upside down."

During the Second World War, Art was a Navy diver stationed in Brooklyn. After that he went to work for the Pere Marquette Railroad in Michigan. We would visit him in his office. It had a big glass door and a rolltop desk. Then he became some kind of executive at Mac-O-Lack Paints in Detroit. At the time, these details seemed tediously normal, insignificant, unimportant. Everyone knew them. That's just what Art did, that's just who he was. But now, over the years, these tiny "fragments" have become extraordinary. Do you hear me? He worked for the Pere Marquette Railroad. Like anything assembled over time, it appreciates, if not in actual value, then in absolute meaning.

He was my father's best man and got him into collecting stamps, too. Since my dad had been a chief pharmacist's mate in the Navy, he saved Red Cross and health stamps. It was only a matter of time before I became a collector of United States commemoratives. From there I moved on to what philatelists call "topicals," stamps with a common theme. I was eleven years old. I chose railroad trains.

I remember the quiet, evening pleasure of completing "sets," of conning my grandfather into taking me to the stamp store, of sitting with my father and tracking the value of my "investments" in the big Scott's catalogue. But above all, I remember the aesthetic joy of arranging (and rearranging) the little colored squares of perforated, gummed paper which could be maneuvered into so many different designs on the pages of my album. Each new configuration gave another nuance of meaning to every individual stamp.

I had forgotten all about my boyhood hobby until I recently found myself waiting in line at the post office. My eye caught one of those displays promoting United States commemorative issues. The poster said something like: "Experience the joy of stamp collecting." When my turn came to mail my package, I surprised myself by asking for a half sheet of stamps, each featuring a different jazz musician. It was as if the clerk were dispensing my own boyhood at 32¢ a pop. I hadn't bought commemoratives for forty years.

One evening, when I was home on vacation from college and Art had been hospitalized, the phone rang. My father held the receiver and said, "Yes, I understand. Thank you." His face was ashen. He hung up, turned to me and said two of the saddest words I've ever heard. To this day I cannot say them without getting a lump in my throat. He said: "Art's dead."

The stories in our lives are like pages of a stamp album. We find ourselves collecting and reassembling ordinary, even trivial, pieces of our childhood, trying, through different re-arrangements, to comprehend their meaning. Perhaps if I put these on this page and move those to another, then add one from the stock book, the page will look right and finally make sense. That's what we do. We take memories which are only distilled stories, add new ones, and, in so doing, redefine their meaning and the shape of our lives.

Professor Moshe Idel of the Hebrew University in Jerusalem has observed that, when recited in the proper manner, ancient text becomes an invocation, a conjuration, that brings about the experience it describes. It is no longer ancient history nor a metaphor for something else, but its re-creation; when performed enthusiastically, the text includes the experience itself.

I'LL TELL YOU A STORY. It's only the memory of a question and about where the question first hit me. I was in high school. My mother was driving me over to Northland Shopping Center. We were going south on Greenfield Highway just across from the old Marathon gas station on Nine Mile Road when it dawned on me that there was an ultimate question: What is the meaning of life? For a moment, I actually considered the possibility that I was the first one ever to have asked it.

My friends, however, had reached identical conclusions for themselves. The same question apparently teased everyone. It could take many forms: What am I doing here? Or: What am I supposed to be doing here? Or: Why am I able to ask this question? Or: Why am I unable to answer it? (The Kabbalists—who had a big head start—say that the ultimate question is simply, "Who?") I suppose that one of the main reasons I became a rabbi is because rabbis have permission to be with people during the most transformative moments of their lives and are even expected to help them make those moments coherent and meaningful.

THE FOLLOWING STORIES ATTEMPT TO CHIP AWAY at a piece of The Question. With one exception, which is obviously fantasy, they are all true; they either happened to me, or, in a few cases, to someone I know. They recount ordinary events. And yet, in one way or another, each one has its own upside down airplane, a misprint, an accident revealing the presence of something more, something sacred.

These stories begin with the discovery of reverence. This guides us back to our place in a galaxy of generations. The third section moves beyond family and out into a community where responsible deeds are the price of admission. Finally, we become aware that everything is connected to everything else through invisible lines of connection. There is only one great, luminous organism.

1. REVERENCE

Bears

THE FIRST TIME MY WIFE KAREN AND I were up in the mountains of Montana, we were awed and even a little frightened by the scale and power of the wilderness. Whether buildings or bridges or even hiking trails, the creations of human beings seemed by comparison precariously inadequate, hopelessly finite, fragile. Back East, nature must be preserved and revered. High in the Rockies, it was the opposite. Here we had to be wary of nature lest, in a blind moment, she consume us all. Everywhere, signs warned of bears. They can run, swim and climb faster than any human being. And they have been known to attack without provocation. Stories circulated about an unwary hiker just a few months ago who. . . .

Karen and I drove up to the end of the road at Two Medicine Lake, where there is a log cabin, general store and a little boat which can ferry you to the trailhead on the far shore. Inside, watching hummingbirds dart to and fro around a feeder, having a cup of coffee, I met Charlie Slocum, a retired biology teacher from Minnesota, who spends his summers working for the National Park Service. In the pristine Eden air, I understood why he had returned now for a score of summers. But I was also more than casually concerned about being eaten by a grizzly.

"Get many bears up here, do you?" I asked.

"Sometimes we get quite a few."

"How 'bout on that easy trail around the lake over there? Any chance of running into any this morning—so near the store...?"

He paused long enough to hear the question behind the question and took a slow sip of his coffee. "If I could tell you for sure there wouldn't be any bears, it wouldn't be a wilderness now would it?"

I thanked him for his candor and we went on our hike. Maybe that is all it ever comes down to: You can walk where things are predictable—or you can enter the wilderness. Without the wilderness, there can be neither reverence nor revelation.

The Hidden Signature

I REMEMBER THE FIRST COMPUTER GAME WE EVER GOT. Since hardly anyone owned computers in those days, you had to use your television set for a monitor. By plugging a cable into the antenna jack, you turned the TV into a primitive video arcade. Then, you could play ping pong—in monochrome. You operated a little paddle that moved up and down along one side of the screen. The ball, actually a white square, moved horizontally. With enough coordination, you could get your paddle to intersect its trajectory, whereupon you heard the game's sole sound effect: "Bip." And so it went: "Bip. Bip. Bip." After you got good at it, you could crank up the speed: "Bip. Bip. Bip. Bip. Bip. Bip." People in our home, who shall remain nameless, played it for hours.

A few years later, Atari became the rage. As I recall Atari initially had four different games. My favorite was called *Adventure*. It was your basic "dungeons and dragons" genre, with different castles and rooms, a key, hidden doorways, a bat that could steal the key, even whole areas where the obstacles were invisible.

Our whole family really got into it. The kids, of course, quickly surpassed their parents. They would come home from school with new tips and tricks. Some of them were even "undocumented," which is computer-talk for saying that such maneuvers were not written down in any manual. One of the most amazing came home from junior high with my daughter: In a particular place inside the "black castle," the diligent searcher could find a small white dot that was too small to be noticeable as a normal game object. Indeed, if you did find it you would think it was only a glitch in your video monitor.

By taking this dot back to the starting screen however, you could enter a hidden, otherwise inaccessible room. Entering the room had absolutely nothing to do with playing the game. All you would find in the room was a rainbow and the name of the person who invented the game. For all I know, every computer programmer does something like this. Somewhere, behind some hidden wall, available only to the initiated, there is another room. And in that room is the name of the artist.

What I want to know is: If the signature of the Creator is not just in some hidden room but in every created thing, why can't we see it?

I once heard of a man whose dental work made it possible for him to actually hear radio broadcasts. Somehow the combination of fillings in his teeth accidentally turned his mouth into a primitive receiver. But he found the sounds so distracting that he had the fillings replaced. The radio signals were still there, he just chose not to hear them any more.

Virtual Reality

ONE OF MY SONS BROUGHT HOME A NEW COMPUTER GAME. This was not one of those video arcade contraptions with primitive little animated characters chasing one another around the screen or space ships shooting at alien invaders. It didn't even require split-second visual reflexes. "It is a new breed," he told me, "called virtual reality." You play it by "entering" it. Your only chance at winning is by imagining that you are actually inside it. Instead of asking, "How do I win this game?" you ask, "What would I do if I really lived in this world?"

At the beginning of this game (called "Myst"), you look at the screen and find yourself on an island. There's a dock, a forest, buildings, stairways. The graphics and sound effects are impressive and convincing. There are no instructions, no rules. You "go" places by aiming a little pointing finger and clicking. You can look up and down, turn around, climb stairs, wander all around the place. Everywhere your curiosity leads you, there are things to discover, learn and remember. There are machines you can operate, a library full of books you can open and read. After a while, the dedicated player will discover how to leave the island and go to other mysterious places. Devotees say the game is properly played over weeks and even months.

And the purpose of it all? Why, of course: To figure out what you're doing there. But to do that, you must first figure out how the place works.

What fascinates me here is not yet another sophisticated and clever way to waste time in front of the computer screen. (I can do that with File Manager.) It is the concept of a game whose purpose is for the player to discover the purpose. Virtual reality, schmirtual reality, this is *no* game. What's going on here? Why am I here? Are there any rules? What are they? How does my behavior affect what is going on?

Upon hearing about all this, Alan Feldman, a friend who is a professor of English, suggested that it seemed a lot like childhood. I'd go farther. It may be a lot like adulthood, too. We all find ourselves in "this world" and the "object" seems to be to figure out what we're doing here. Unfortunately, most of the ways one thing is connected to or dependent upon another thing are not immediately apparent. If we live long enough, take careful notes and listen to those who have gone before us, we stand a chance.

After all, meaning is primarily a matter of relationship. If something is connected to absolutely nothing—symbolically, linguistically, physically, psychologically—it is literally meaning-less. And in the same way, if something is connected to everyone and everything, it would be supremely meaning-full. I suppose it would be God: The "One" through whom everything is connected to everything else, the Source of all meaning. Religious traditions are the collected "rules of the game." They tell us how the world works. And if you "play by them," you are rewarded (hopefully before it is time to leave) with an understanding of why you are here; with what is otherwise known as the meaning of life.

While my new virtual reality computer game may be infuriatingly intricate and frustrating, at least I have the comfort of knowing that it was designed by someone. I may not be clever enough to figure out its purpose, but it does have one. Its rules can be learned; it can be completed; it has an end. Life, on the other hand, comes with no such implicit guarantee, and its time frame and playing field are literally beyond our comprehension.

What if there were a virtual reality computer game that was programmed to approximate real life? If you could design such a program, what would be "the object"? The way I see it there are only a few rules.

THE FIRST RULE OF THE GAME OF LIFE is that you cannot decide when to begin playing. One day, out of the blue, you realize that you're playing. Someone or something else determined when the game would begin. And it wasn't your parents. They may have known about the birds and the bees and even set out to conceive a child, but they didn't have a clue it was going to be you. And now that they've had a chance to meet you, while they most likely love you, they'd probably have picked someone else. In religious language, this means that you are a creature. Someone *else* made you. And you are neither its partner nor its puppet: You are its manifestation, its agent, its child.

The second rule is that you cannot decide when to *stop* playing the game, either. One day, out of the blue, you're dead. For a slogan on the box of the game of "Life," we could use something I saw on a T-shirt: "Life: You're not going to make it out alive!" That means there's no way you can "win" the game by staying in it forever. No matter how many points, toys, honors, conquests, dollars you accumulate, sooner than anyone expects or wants, the game is abruptly over. You hear a little chime, maybe a buzzer, the keyboard freezes, the screen goes blank. The game ends without warning. Nothing you acquire, accomplish, or believe will have any effect whatsoever on when the game ends. But there's good news: Dying does not mean you lose. It's what you do *before* you die that determines whether or not you win when you die.

The third rule—just to keep you on your toes—is that each player is issued apparently random, undeserved gifts and handicaps throughout the progress of the game. Figuring out why you got the combination package you did transforms all disabilities into gifts, just as refusing to figure out why you were issued what you received, transforms all gifts into disabilities. My father used to say that all men are not created equal. Some get dealt a full house; others, a pair of twos. The question therefore is not whether you deserve the hand you were dealt, but how you choose to play it.

The fourth rule is that points are awarded whenever you can discern the presence, or the signature, of the Creator, and then act so as to help others see it too. The signature is not just in objects, but in actions and thoughts and feelings; not just in sunshine and happiness, but in agony, struggle and death. Remember: Finding the signature and then acting in such a way as to help others find it too, is the only way to accumulate game points.

And the last rule is that everything is connected to everything else. Therefore, life is supercharged, permeated and over-brimming with purpose and meaning. Most of the time we are oblivious to it. We go about our lives as if every event were an accident. And then something happens and we see the connection. For a just moment it is unmistakable. We are astonished that we couldn't see it until now. All Creation is one great unity. There are no coincidences.

Throughout all Creation, just beneath the surface, joining each person to every other person and to every other thing in a luminous organism of sacred responsibility, we discover invisible lines of connection.

Now *that's* my idea of a game.

This Is Your Life

WHEN I WAS GROWING UP, there was a TV show during which they'd bring an unsuspecting soul out of the studio audience and tell his or her life story. It was creatively called, "This Is Your Life." The master of ceremonies would recount part of a story and from offstage you would hear a little old lady say, "I remember the way you used to sit in the back row of my geometry class and throw paper airplanes at the little blonde girl across the aisle." Whereupon the guest of honor would say something like, "Oh my God, it's Mrs. Connley!" And Mrs. Connley would come out from behind the curtain and they would hug and usually cry. The master of ceremonies would tell a few more stories and introduce a few more mystery guests until the past joined the present and the guest's life was told. Then, the show was over. It took a half hour.

Deprived of a television program, the rest of us are left instead to review our lives through a hodgepodge of stories that describe what we think we have done and what we think has been done to us. Only rarely does it make sense.

THERE IS A FASCINATING PASSAGE near the end of Deuteronomy: "And not until this day has God given you a heart to understand, eyes to see, or ears to hear. I led you through the wilderness forty years and the clothes on your back did not wear out…" In other words, for the four prior decades the children of Israel had wandered clueless around the wilderness and never had to shop for clothes. Sounds odd, if you ask me.

Simcha Bunam, one of the early Hasidic masters, explains that this passage means that the Israelites did not understand what God did during those forty years because everything that happened was unique to that particular time. There had never been anything like it before; there would never be anything like it again. The wandering Israelites of Sinai never figured out what was going on because it never dawned on them that they were players in a sacred story.

At the end of forty years, however, the Jews realized that religious history was about to be clothed in their deeds, made from whatever they had done. Not only from the holy moments, but from the mundane, the wayward, even the sinful moments as well. Imagine, ultimate truth clothed in the stories of your life. (This, indeed, is your life.)

Now if you protest that the deeds of your life are simply too irreligious to be included in such a holy book, take comfort in the behavior of everyone from Adam through Joshua: Murderers, lechers, liars, cheats, thieves. As Hanan Brichto, professor of Bible at Hebrew Union College, used to quip, there's no one in the Hebrew Bible you'd want your kid to grow up to be like.

And the wilderness generation, that wacky, zany band of irreligious forty-year wanderers—who, with their own eyes, saw the Red Sea split and Moses ascend Mount Sinai, who ate manna for breakfast and quail for supper—these were the ones who built the golden calf, denied God at every opportunity, begged to go back to Egypt and committed adultery with every tribe they met. These exemplary spiritual specimens were privileged to have the serial rights to their life story chosen for the script of the most holy document every recorded.

So there's hope for you and me, yet. But alas, for most of us, only at the end of forty years do we begin to understand that even *our* life stories are sacred, that no television show could possibly comprehend them, and that God has been involved all along. Reverence is the only option.

Federal Express

ONE OF THE LAST THINGS YOU GET TO LOOK AT as an author, before your book goes to press, is something called "proofs." They are part of the error-checking mechanism.

Now people in the book business, like people in most businesses, are always looking for ways to make their jobs go quickly. So they often unceremoniously shorten the titles of books to just a word or two. Since the book which I had just finished would have one of the longer titles of any book ever published, it was an easy victim to such abbreviating. The full title was: *God Was in This Place and I, i Did Not Know.* Eleven words, which usually would get abbreviated to simply, "God Was in This Place." On at least one occasion, it has been further distilled by a mailroom clerk to just "God." This is all a roundabout way of explaining how the Federal Express package that arrived at my home from the publisher of the book was labeled, "God Proofs."

My kids, who were home to sign for the package, telephoned me at the office at once to announce—not without some mischievous glee—that what I had been working on and waiting for my whole adult life had just arrived via FedEx.

"It's finally here, dad. 'God Proofs.'"

"Is there a return address?" I asked, wondering whether heaven had a zip code.

If a proof for God could come in the mail, what would it look like? It would be a book containing all the stories of your life. But because they are all holy stories concealing myriad lights, ordinary words cannot contain them. The stories are necessarily fluid because each new page redefines the meaning of all the previous stories—just as each new deed ripples back through all the previous deeds. This is your life.

You Are Here

As a birthday present not long ago, I got a sailor's hand-held navigational computer. It's not much bigger than a pack of cigarettes. On only a few AA batteries, the gadget's antenna can pick up the signals of satellites orbiting the earth. Once it gets three clear signals, it makes a "fix," and, within half a football field's length of accuracy, you can know where you are anywhere on the surface of the earth. And then you'll know how to steer toward your destination. Well, sort of.

It turns out that knowing how to get somewhere requires a lot more than simply knowing your latitude and longitude coordinates. In addition, you must have a map or a chart and—here is the part we often forget—you also need to know where something *else* is on the map. It could be a lighthouse, the direction of North, or, for that matter, if you were looking at one of those information boards in a shopping mall, where another store is *in relation to* where you are standing. You might say that there's more to getting somewhere than simply knowing where you are. Orientation also requires some *other* fixed point. I was a crew member on a sailboat sailing up Lake Michigan through the night when I learned this.

At such a time, there is only you, the other members of the crew and the boat, patiently working her way through the waves and the night. Deprived of light, the effects of wind and waves can only be felt. The sea seems bigger than in the daylight. After a while, you get confused about where you end and the boat begins and where the boat ends and the water begins.

Ahead of you in the evening lies the last thin strip of twilight, a barely visible line of dark purple separating the upper waters from the lower waters. Then, without any sound of protest, it dissolves. Gone. Now the only visible remains of the terrestrial world are in the distance behind: The slowly sinking, ten-second, white flash from the lighthouse on Point Betsy. That bright burst of light, higher than the horizon, will faithfully continue to provide a line of position. You may not know exactly how far away you are, but you do know, at least, that you are somewhere on that line.

As you sail farther and farther into the empty black, even Point Betsy misses a beat. Like a candle or a life going out, she flickers. Then she, too, is gone. Blackness everywhere. With her, you were oriented. Without her, you are not only alone in the dark, you cannot even be certain where you are.

Each lighthouse has its own distinctive pattern of flashes, a coded light-message which enables an approaching mariner to identify his location on the chart. They are all recorded in *The Coast Pilot Light List*. They are all that any lighthouse ever says: "This is who I am. This is who I am. This is who I am."

Pound of Heaven

A COLLEAGUE OF MINE, WHO IS AN ORTHODOX JEW, grew up in a *musar yeshiva*, a religious academy. *Musar* means scolding or ethical pietism. It connotes a personal code which is rigorous, even harsh. A few years ago, over kosher Chinese food, my friend told me of an exercise some of the older students in the *yeshiva* had devised which still strikes me as both beautiful and disturbing.

The goal was to get yourself to a place where you were immune from ordinary social rewards and punishments, strip yourself of ego and attain true humility, even equanimity. This, some of the students were convinced, required immunity even from feelings which betrayed the presence of ego: Pride and shame. As an exercise, they would send someone into a hardware store to order one pound of *yirat shamayim*, or "reverence before heaven."

"What's that you say? *Yirat shamayim*? You want a pound of it!" the store's proprietor would howl. "Ha, ha, ha! You stupid fool. You dumb yokel. You can't buy reverence by the pound. Hey, why don't you try the post office across the street. I think they have some. Ha, ha, ha! Get outta here!"

REVERENCE BEFORE HEAVEN. Amazing grace. It is a way of understanding your place within Creation. It means that you see yourself as part of some greater organism, that the presence of something very holy (which some call "God") permeates and unifies all being. It means that you play a

35

sacred role in Creation's unfolding. And that, when viewed from a point of high enough vantage, everything is revealed to be in the hands of God, as in the Yiddish saying, *Alles ist Gott*, "It's all God."

I don't know if I would be able to pass such a test. I'm not even sure I'd want the distinction. But hearing about it made me wonder: Where *would* you go to get reverence before heaven, anyway? You can't buy it by the pound, but how *do* you acquire it? And when you have it, how do you know? And once you know, what do you *do*?

West 28th Street

YOU DON'T HAVE TO GO TO JERUSALEM OR MECCA to make a pilgrimage. A few years ago, I made a pilgrimage by taking a taxi to a six-story, 19th century building in midtown Manhattan. On the outside of the building were decades of different colored, flaking paint, graffiti, fire escapes and a sign for the "Acme International Toy Importers" or something like that. Trash littered the sidewalk. The double doors atop the front stairway suggested this was once a residence. I did not go inside. I just stood on the opposite side of the street looking at the building, for I had come to pay my respects.

A few months before this little trip, I had been in the National Archives in Washington. With some diligence and a lot of luck, I had managed to locate page seven of the Manifest of Alien Passengers of the U.S. Immigration Officer at the Port of New York for October 10, 1905. At the top, it said that twenty-seven days earlier, the steamship Georgia had set sail from Trieste. On line #187, neatly penned by an immigration officer, was the name of one Yakob Kuzhner; age, 32; married, yes; occupation, tailor; able to read and write, yes; nationality, Russian; race, Hebrew. Then, at the end of the line: Whither going, 15 West 28th Street, New York. My father, his memory is a blessing, would not yet be born for six years.

So, Yakob Kuzhner, my *zeyde*, my grandpa, *this* is where you landed. And here I am, in a blue blazer with a Filene's Basement Polo necktie and a satchel full of my rabbinic students' papers, trying hopelessly to look inconspicuous long enough to savor the closing of a lifetime circle.

Oi zeyde, oh grandpa, we both came a long way. I, the first son of your ninth and youngest child; I, your fourteenth grandchild, remember how, when I couldn't have been more than eight years old, we sat on your second-story sun porch in Detroit, and you got down on your haunches and, over Grandma's protests, held onto a chair, extended first one leg straight out and then the other and showed me how to dance the *kazachok* so, as you said, I would know how to have a good time at weddings.

A voice from behind me broke my reverie on West 28th Street: "Hey man, you lost?"

"No, I'm cool. Thanks."

But it was a lie.

Fear of Dying

SEVERAL YEARS AGO, DURING A MEETING of the board of directors of my congregation, I realized that I was wiping my eye glasses every few minutes. It was a good meeting: People argued fair and about important religious matters, and even I managed not to say anything too stupid. It wasn't until well into the meeting that I realized that the smudge I was trying to wipe off my glasses wasn't on my glasses: It was on my left eye. It appeared almost imperceptibly, painlessly, quickly.

When it didn't go away after a few days, I called my ophthalmologist. To my concern, he wanted me to come in right away.

"It's probably just a 'floater,'" said my wife. "Don't worry, I'm sure it's nothing."

And since, as an adult, I had never been hospitalized, I figured she must be right.

But, after a very thorough examination, my physician told me that there was something going on with my optic nerve which he could not explain and that he wanted me to see an ophthalmic neurologist in the city.

"What's wrong?" I asked.

"It's probably nothing. Just a precaution."

"Against what?" I pushed.

He listed several maladies, but none were grave enough to warrant the urgency I thought I detected in his voice. After some very frontal, direct questions such as, "Give me the worst possible scenario," he confessed that my symptoms could be the early signs of a brain lesion.

I felt what I can only call "a trembling deep inside me." And I remember thinking: So this is how it happens. One day, I'm well. Then, suddenly and almost gracefully, I'm in possession of an all-consuming new piece of information: The probable cause of my imminent death. One minute I'm preoccupied by a thousand daily tasks. And the next, it's as if some hand from out of nowhere had swept everything off the game board and onto the floor and replaced all my affairs with a medical diagnosis.

WHEN I WAS GROWING UP IN DETROIT, the rabbi assigned to the youth group was Harold Hahn. He was a good rabbi and went on to assume a major pulpit. One morning, while shaving, he noticed that the razor kept slipping from his hand. Within a short time, he was dead of a brain tumor. I saw him at a convention just before he was taken and he shared with me a passage from Kierkegaard: "A tiger can jump out of the forest at any moment." So that is how it happens. Now I was scheduled for a CAT scan in two days.

Suddenly, everything I did was suffused with meaning. I couldn't take anything for granted. The most trivial sensations became gifts: The smell of my children's hair. The sound of the dog barking. My wife's kiss. The morning coffee. Each was too precious to let go of.

What can I say? I went for the CAT scan. They couldn't find anything. After two decades of studying Jewish mysticism, it was a miracle they could even detect a brain.

The next few weeks brought more tests. All negative. I learned a new word, "idiopathic," which means that the doctors don't exactly know the cause of your malady but that you shouldn't worry. "If you want," one of my physicians said, "you can call it 'optic neuritis,' an inflamed optic nerve."

I got a reprieve. Whoever had pulled my file, must have put it back in the "life" cabinet. Or, as one of my congregants said, "Rabbi, it's just God's way of saying, 'Gottcha!'"

Life, you are so sweet. Would that there be some way of getting to that heightened gratitude for life without the terror. I suppose that when organized religion works (which is more often than many of us admit), such an appreciation is given.

Setting Out

SOONER OR LATER, THE LAND ALWAYS SLOPES toward the sea. This time it was down the narrow street leading from our rooming house to the launch dock. We could not tell whether the morning mist would burn off or become day-long drizzle. Some weathered New England cottages, which had heard it all before, leaned over the street trying to eavesdrop. But there was nothing new to hear. It was only I who was afraid he was going to die. It's like that whenever I set out for the boat.

My friend, Louis, who has sailed across the Atlantic and is probably the best sailor I know, was with me. But this time it was my boat and I was the captain.

"Nervous?" he asked with an understanding smile.

"Actually, I'm terrified," I joked.

But we both knew it was not entirely a joke. "That's the reason long-distance sailors stopping at an island to take on provisions don't spend any more time than absolutely necessary," he consoled. "It's never spoken, but they're afraid they won't have the nerve to get back on the boat again."

THE OCEAN IS VERY BIG; the boat is very small. Once the voyage begins, you can't get off: Your feet won't touch the bottom. You cannot hold back a wave or redirect the wind. You are dependent on your own skill at balancing the force of the wind and the force of the sea. Somehow, you must persuade them to cooperate with one another and, as a token of their gratitude, accept a free ride in repayment. Even setting foot on the boat and casting off requires something like faith. It may be like that with standing in the presence of the Holy One: This One deals not only life, but also death. When the voyage or the wedding or the worship service is done, we return to the land and its fixedness with a heightened appreciation for simply still being alive.

Hopefully, most of the time, a brush with death turns out to be a brush with life. Come to think of it, I guess you'd have to say that *all* of the times—except the *last* one—brushes with death turn out to be brushes with life. People seem to require dramatically varying amounts of "trembling" to remind themselves that they might die so that they can realize they're really alive. Kafka said that the meaning of life is that it ends.

Riding the Golden Camel

WE HAD COME TO THE MOUNT OF OLIVES in Jerusalem to see that magnificent view of the old city that is available only from its summit. We had also come to indulge some people in our party, whose hearts were set on a camel ride. We watched them get their money's worth as the beast lurched first up and forward, then higher and backward, and finally forward and level, at last. The city of gold spread out before us. Just in front of us was a valley where the parched stones of a graveyard fought with clumps of grass and shrubs for space. Bored with camel rides and panoramas, my attention was easily caught by a dozen or so people, slowly moving below through the valley. They were dressed in black and carrying what looked like a tabletop with something on it, covered by a cloth. Looking closely, I realized that the object on the table was a lifeless human body and that I was watching a funeral.

"Where is the coffin?" I asked my Israeli friend.

"In the holy city," he replied, "there are no coffins. The earth herself is the box. Watch what happens now."

The mourners gathered around the freshly dug grave. They were much too far away to hear, but I presume there were, as we rabbis say, "some words," and then, while the tabletop was set at the edge of the grave, a member of the *hevra kaddisha*, the burial society, actually climbed down into the pit. The cords which held the corpse to the board were loosened, the board carefully teeter-tottered halfway over the foot of the grave, and, as those on top slowly continued to raise their end, the man in the grave slid his hands under the shoulders of the body and gently guided it to its final resting place in the holy earth. The member of the *hevra* was helped up and out. The grave was filled. The mourners formed two lines. The camel ride was over.

2. INHERITANCE

What It's All About

I WAS SITTING BY MYSELF in a crowded downtown steak house waiting for an old friend to join me for dinner. The waiter had just brought me a glass of wine and I was going over photocopies of some Hasidic texts I planned to study with my rabbinic students the next morning. Despite the clatter and the noise and trying to concentrate on my reading, I became aware that the two young men behind me were talking about how one of them recently became a father.

"...Ya know, I look at that little baby and it comes to me, this is really what it's all about."

That's all I heard. It was enough.

It reminded me of the wedding of the daughter of a friend. During a lull in the commotion, my friend mused the same thing: "This is really what it's all about, isn't it."

"Sure is," I answered, but now I've got to wondering: What does "This is *really* what *it's* all about" really mean? Are other things not what it's all about? What is "it"? And "about" what?

THERE USED TO BE THIS DANCE we did in junior high school. It was a "mixer," that's a euphemism for everybody could do it. Dweeby kids, dorky kids, nerdy kids and popular kids—like you and me. Everyone formed a big circle. There was someone in the center (usually an English teacher) who led it. She would say, "You put your right hand in, you take your right hand out, you put your right hand in and you shake it all about." For those of you from Mars, the dance was called the Hokey Pokey. It went on like that, each time featuring a different part of the human anatomy. There are a lot of parts. And young adolescents take great pleasure in shaking them, especially while they are surreptitiously watching what other young adolescents look like while they are doing the same thing. The dance ended with everyone complying with and singing the final instruction: "You put your whole self in, you take your whole self out. You put your whole self in and you shake it all about. You do the Hokey Pokey, and you shake yourself about. And *that's what it's all about.*"

So *that's* what it's all about! You put your whole self in, you take your whole self out; you put your whole self in and you shake it all about. The idea is that by doing whatever you're doing with all of you, you can then take all of you out. The trick is how to do both.

It is possible to put your whole self into many things that are gratifying, beautiful and even important but which, in retrospect, we realize are *not* what it's all about. We confuse the great and transforming joy that usually accompanies life's milestones with being what it's all about. This is because they are so intense that we must put our whole self into them. But if we allow them to become the goal, then they are only diversions. Putting your whole self in and shaking it all about is important (and usually a lot of fun, too) but it is not enough. You also have to take your whole self out. You must also go beyond your self, transcend your self.

Only then can we can glimpse a bigger picture and our place in it. Such times put our lives in a larger system of meaning. In one way or another, they all involve separating

from our parents, or remembering our place in the generations or realizing that we have been born and that we will
die. Such moments are "what it's all about." They put our
whole self in the circle. And as we watch dumbfounded while
we dissolve, for a moment, there is only radiance.

Homecoming

WE SPEND OUR LIVES TRYING TO GET FAR AWAY from our parents and to keep our children close. But since everyone is both a child and a parent of the next generation, you don't have to be a rocket scientist to figure out that we have a problem here. Lots of parents wanting to keep their kids close. Lots of kids trying to get away. Lots of kids wishing they could go home, but not being able to stand it when they get there. Lots of parents eager for their kids to go back to school, but not being able to stand it once they're gone.

It's crazy. Like dogs, they love to jump into the car and as soon as they're in the car, they love to jump out of the car. Comedian Gary Shandling says he just leaves both car doors open. They jump in. They jump out. It can go on for hours. We have it worse. We do it with our parents for our whole lives.

I remember how almost twenty years ago Karen and I hid at the window watching our oldest child wait at the edge of the driveway for the big yellow school bus. The bus was so big, she literally had to climb up on the first step. We cried. The other day, she called from Los Angeles where she is a graduate rabbinic student. She wanted to tell us what she was preaching to the folks where she is an intern. I asked her to send us a copy.

"Why?" she asked.

"So we can put it on the refrigerator next to your report card," I joked. (But it wasn't a joke.)

I remember the first week I spent at college. I took the Baltimore & Ohio sleeper from Detroit down to Cincinnati. I had to register for courses, move into a dorm room, meet classmates, open my first checking account, buy textbooks, attend orientations, do homework—and, of course, set the world on fire. There was no turning back. I remember sitting at my desk, watching the cars go by on Clifton Avenue, thinking how nice it would be to be back home, but deciding that since it was going to be like this for the rest of my life, I'd better get used to it. But I cried anyway. Then I went to bed.

How could I have known that at that very moment my parents also held one another and wept. Why do people cry about everything they have prayed for?

THE FIRST TIME I CAME HOME from the University of Cincinnati was Thanksgiving. The night air was cold with the intimation of snow. One of the guys in my dorm drove this old Citroen which had hydraulic suspension. When you turned on the ignition, the car made a funny hissing sound and raised itself a few inches. He was from Toronto and had to drive through Detroit on his way home. Two other guys and I hitched a ride with him. Long sections of the route were down the main streets of Ohio farm towns, so the trip took over eight hours and I didn't get home until after ten.

As we pulled into the driveway, I saw my mother standing on the front porch. She was dressed awfully nice for a Wednesday evening at home. I am sure of this because she was wearing this garish, gray and pink blouse with rhinestones on it. It was the only time I ever saw her wear it. I had given it to her for her birthday the year before and had forgotten all about it. And now, there she was, on our front porch in the middle of the night, wearing it like a lighthouse guiding the Citroen's precious cargo home. Even my father had positioned himself in a chair he hated, but which did offer a commanding view of the driveway. Working the crossword puzzle, he looked up for a moment. My mother walked out to the car and held me at arm's length so as to take all of me in and examine the merchandise, this adventurer from Ohio who had come forth from her body.

"My God, why didn't you call? We were worried something had happened to you. Would your friends like to come inside for some coffee and some fresh baked pie?" (My mother had never baked a thing in her life!)

No, thank you, they were already very late and eager to get back on the road.

I took my valise and went inside.

At the time, I didn't understand about family and the simple power of going away and coming back. I now realize that this setting out and returning home again is a kind of dance we do with our Source and our Destiny. We spend our lives learning and rehearsing the steps, first as children, then from the other side as the parent generation.

If we learn it right, when our time comes to die we are not afraid. It is not unlike the last words of the Hasidic master Rabbi Simcha Bunam, who, as he lay dying, took his wife's hand and said, "Why are you crying? My whole life was only that I might learn how to die."

Espionage

THE WAY MY DESK IS SITUATED, when the door to my office at the synagogue is open, I can see the corner where the main hallway intersects the corridor that leads to the classrooms and the preschool. It's a good view.

The other day, unaware of my gaze, I saw a young mother, with an infant propped on her hip, leaning around the corner which is coincidentally right in front of my door. At first, I thought she was having trouble balancing the baby, but then I saw her straighten up, bring her head back and disappear. It was just a glimpse and I only half-processed the scene. But a few minutes later, she did it again. By the third time, I was a shameless voyeur.

Sure enough, in a few more minutes she reappeared, surreptitiously looking down the corridor. What was going on? And then I heard the voices of the preschool children at their first week of school. Now I understood. This woman was watching her child, but she didn't want her child to see her—and I was secretly watching her. Then she saw me. Embarrassed to be caught, she offered one of those apologetic faces we make when we fear we might appear stupid. I whispered, "It's very beautiful—what you're doing. Why don't you come inside the doorway of my office where you can get a better view." But she was new to our community (and probably thought I'd make her memorize a page of Talmud or something), so she politely declined and retreated to the other end of the building.

I saw her later in the morning and tried a consolation. "It only gets worse when they get older. Then you have to employ much more sophisticated means of surveillance and if you're caught, children in their twenties and thirties have been known to go underground for years. Sometimes the only information a parent can get comes from a traveler who happened to see your kid in some far away city or country or—may God grant them eternal happiness—actually took them out for a meal, pumped them full of questions and secretly tape recorded their answers."

It occurs to me that hide-and-seek is more than a game. It may be a rehearsal for living in a family.

Wool Pants

WHEN I WAS A LITTLE BOY growing up in Detroit, my family attended a big cathedral of a Reform temple. The sunlight streamed in through the stained glass windows, there were more light bulbs in the chandeliers than stars in the sky and you could actually feel the organ music with your whole body. We used to tease the organist, a friend of our family's, that he played too loud and nicknamed him "Thunder Foot."

On the Jewish New Year, no matter how early my parents and my brother and I arrived in the Main Sanctuary, or, as we called it, the "Big Room," my grandfather was always there waiting for us. (This was especially surprising to me because we had driven him there in our car.) There he sat like a proper German gentleman, second aisle on the right, fourth row. There weren't assigned pews, but we always sat there: It was *our* place.

Everyone was all dressed up. My aunt called it *fapitzed*, which meant, I think, wearing more expensive clothes than my aunt could afford. It seemed very important to see everyone and to be seen by everyone. In fact, the main thing everyone seemed to care about was that a lot of people would see what they were wearing. It wasn't one of religion's most sublime expressions, but something sacred was going on.

Every few years, I would get a new outfit for temple. As far as I can tell, it always had wool pants which seemed to have two properties. First, each trouser leg had a crease down the middle and, if I wasn't careful when I sat down, the crease would disappear at the knee and my mother would get mad at me. The other thing about wool pants was that they all seemed to be made with thousands of perspiration-activated, microscopic needles. This meant that as soon as it got hot, they itched and the boy couldn't sit still. The creases would start to disappear. And then my mother would yell at me. (When I got older, an allergist informed me that I was mildly allergic to wool. So it goes.)

Every year, I would complain, "Ma, what's the big deal about what I'm wearing? I don't care what your friends think I look like." But every year we would go to temple where my brother and I would be inspected by every Jew in Michigan, all of whom seemed to know my parents and cared that my wool pants were neatly creased.

"My, how he's grown," one would sigh.

"What a lovely outfit. Where did you find it?" approved another.

"My pants itch!" I would murmur.

"Stand still!"

WITH THE ADVENT OF POLYESTER and a half dozen years, my complaint matured into an adolescent disgust with facade which, I now suspect, may be the first glimmer of religious maturity: "All anybody seems to care about here is how they're dressed. This isn't religion; it's a fashion parade. Why does everyone only care how they look?"

Of course organized religion itches. It is trying to hold a crease in life. But what most adolescents fail to understand is the religious power of simply being seen and looking good in the "Big Room." It is a way of appearing before God who we suspect is not beneath looking through the eyes of the community. Being seen by the congregation is like being seen by God. All those souls, together in that sanctuary, make something religious happen.

Brotherly Love

ACTUALLY, considering that over six years separate us, my younger brother and I are very much alike. He is also a rabbi and serves a congregation about the same size as mine. He weighs more, but I have less hair. We have been confused for twins. Steve confessed that recently, when we were in a department store together, he spoke to his own image in a mirror for a second before he realized it wasn't me. I told him I took it as an insult.

The truth is, he is too much like me. He reminds me of myself. We share many of the same faults. But in him, instead of being artfully concealed, integrated into a polished personality (as they are in me), they just lie there for me to observe and detest. The obnoxious things he does on his own don't bother me much. It's the stuff he does that I do *too* that I can't stand. And most of the obnoxious things he does, I do, too. We both learned it from the same parents—except for a few innovations he got straight from me.

We often talk several times a week, but we still find one another unintelligible. I sometimes love him and fantasize going on a long voyage together. Other times, I really wish he'd just leave me alone. What can you do? We're brothers.

ONE SUMMER MORNING NOT LONG AGO, these two sons of Miriam and Aid Kushner were each driving a Toyota. The younger Kushner was driving a Camry sedan; even though it makes him poor, he claims that it makes him feel rich.

The older Kushner was driving a Celica sports coupe. It helps him deal with being over 50. Steve bought his car first, but I have a faster computer with a bigger hard disk. Together with their wives, these brothers were driving down to Cape Cod to take Steven's two little girls out on Uncle Larry's sailboat.

"Slow down or he won't be able to follow you," said Karen.

"Don't worry," I mumbled, "he's been following me for over forty years."

He's always been able to find me—in the supermarket, at the shopping mall, in the park, at school. When he wasn't physically following me, he was psychologically following me, dressing like me, acting like me. Good grief, he was even telling my jokes. My parents said I should feel honored by this attention.

"Imitation is the highest form of compliment," they reminded me.

"I don't want any compliments. Just tell him to leave me alone!"

But it was no use. We may not have been twins, but we were joined at the hip. Stuck with one another.

So here we were doing 65 miles an hour, weaving our way down Route 24 through a construction zone slalom of one million orange barrels, half a million concrete barricades and one thousand trucks when an evil idea came into my head: "Why not just lose him?"

"Whoops! Where'd he go? Gone. Too bad."

But then I heard my mother's voice.

"What do you mean you lost your little brother! You went to the movies together. You were supposed to take care of him. He looks up to you. He was holding your hand. Where is he?"

"I dunno. Maybe he got lost in an alley somewhere, you know, fell in a garbage can. Maybe a big dog ate him. I can't watch him every minute. I guess he's gone forever."

But it didn't work. It never does. No matter how fast I run (or drive) I can't seem to shake him. And the truth is, I don't want to. You see, we are the only ones who are made of Miriam and Aid Kushner. Through us, they will be immortal. Besides, after all these years, I've sort of grown attached to him. He is a good man.

Over my desk at home, I still have the sketch I made on the first day of spring at my grandparents' home when I was 6½ years old. I drew it while I was sitting at the little table in the hallway by the telephone. (In those days, each home had only one phone.) My grandma said, as she handed me a box of colored pencils, "You sit here and draw. When the phone rings, you can be the first to pick it up and find out whether you have a brother or a sister." So I sat there and drew this picture of a little boy on stilts, looking over a fence. The little boy is waving.

Cycle of the Tide

A FEW YEARS AGO, FOR A SUMMER VACATION, we rented a place on Cape Cod. The house wasn't much, but the views were spectacular. Behind the house was a tidal salt marsh. During low tide, all you could see was high grass everywhere and a muddy stream bed. Then somehow, mysteriously, during the five hour and twenty-five minute tidal cycle, the swamp became, silently and imperceptibly, an inland sea eleven feet deep. Our landlord had given us the use of his long dock which ran through the high grass and ended at the creek in the middle. The dock was only a few feet wide and must have been at least fifty yards long. By the time you walked out to the end during a high tide, you felt like you were in another dimension: There was only this thin ribbon of rickety, weathered boards tethering you to land. It was all you had to insulate you from whatever was going on in the atmosphere and in the water. At high tide, on the far end of the dock, misty moonlit nights had a life all their own.

One of the reasons we spent the full summer on the Cape was so our two oldest children would be able to hold down summer-long jobs there and earn money for college. Only after committing ourselves to stay the extra time did we realize that it was costing us more than their combined incomes. At least, Karen and I consoled ourselves, they were learning about fiscal responsibility, even if their parents hadn't.

Because they were working, we didn't see enough of them. But then again, we haven't seen enough of them since they were in grammar school. Like the tidal current behind the house, we would get them like we used to on summer vacation when they were little, filling every minute with an ocean of their presence, hanging around, undecided about what to do with themselves. Then, just as quietly and inexorably, they would be off. And when they got older, if we were lucky, we might catch a fleeting glimpse as they drove to work or called to say they would be spending the night with friends.

Coming home.

Going away.

Coming home again.

Toward the end of our holiday, our middle son, then only a few weeks short of his departure for college, came home late one evening. We were alone together. I had already been through sending our daughter off, but her college was close enough to be within easy driving distance. My son would need to take an airplane. He could not be easily reached (a fact which Karen and I suspected had probably influenced his choice of colleges). We knew we were living through the commencement of another great tidal cycle. If we were lucky, there would be many more summers together. But, no matter how much food you put out on the table, nothing is guaranteed.

Now I'd like you to think that we in the Kushner home never argue or fight or throw soft objects or slam doors in fits of anger. But every now and then, we briefly lapse into what any reasonable observer would properly call "very stupid fights." This is almost always because we are too unimaginative or frightened to realize our deeper feelings. It was just such a stupid fight I picked that night with Zack. As I recollect, it was over the use of the car and all the power and freedom that the use of the car usually symbolizes. We began with what sounded like a reasonable argument.

He said, "I want the car."

I said, "I want the car, too."

He said, "I *really* need it."

"You can't have it."

"But why?"

"Because it's *my* car." (This was very mature.)

Matters got worse and worse. Soon, we were yelling and trying to make one another feel ashamed. Issues, unresolved from years ago, surfaced. We were both fighting with all our strength. I felt my whole body grow tense.

Suddenly, I noticed that my son's eyes were moist with tears. But before I could say anything, he said to me, "Dad, you're crying." And as I blinked the wetness away, I realized he was right. And then we both fell silent. For then we both understood: It hadn't been about the car at all. It was about his going away.

"C'mon," I said, "let's walk out on the dock and look at the water."

"I don't want to."

"Please, just as a favor."

"Look, I love you, but I just don't want to do that now."

"Then why are you putting on your jacket?" I asked.

"Because you'll just make me feel guilty as hell if I don't. C'mon, dad, let's get it over with..."

And so we walked out on the dock and watched the tide ebb away. Summer was almost over.

The Blue Hat

I CAME HOME FROM MY OFFICE to find my wife sitting at the kitchen table in front of the day's mail. She was crying. Before her was an open manila envelope. I guess you'd have to say that the reason for her tears went back almost two decades to the birth of the daughter of friends. They were then living in Princeton and, as luck would have it, I had to be in Philadelphia for a meeting just a few days after the baby was born. Instead of flying, I took the train home to Boston so I could stop and pay my respects to the new little girl.

It was already dark when I arrived. We tiptoed around the crib and whispered so we wouldn't wake the baby. I got all teary eyed when I saw the hopes and pride shining from her parents' faces. I gave them a mobile to hang over the crib and a small wardrobe of hand-me-down baby clothes that our own daughter, Noa, then a world-traveling five years old, had long since outgrown. The assortment included a little, blue and white, winter hat my mother-in-law had knitted. It had a little tassel on the top and on each ear flap hung a cord which could be tied in a bow under the chin—presumably to keep the hat snugly in place in the event of gale force winds.

I had forgotten all about that hat. And now there it was again on the kitchen table. Our friends were cleaning out their attic and thoughtfully returned it to us and, with it, all the memories of our own little girl that were woven within. So I held Karen and now we both cried.

To drive us crazy, when Noa was twenty-one and had just graduated from college, she and a friend decided to travel around the world. Before setting out, she worked as a waitress to earn some money for her trip. To save even more money, she moved back home. This meant there were again more drivers than cars and, once again, arguments about who needed the car more. It seemed self-evident to everyone else that Daddy would simply have to walk the mere mile to work. Sometimes, if I got lucky, I could bum a ride. I grabbed my briefcase and ran out to the car. Noa was already behind the wheel.

She instantly saw the humor of the situation and asked in a maternal, scolding voice, "Why do I always have to wait for you? Did you remember to bring your lunch? I have a very busy day and won't be able to drive it up to school later."

"Yeah," I replied, "I got it but we're outta the applesauce and all I could find was a yucchy pear."

She then proceeded to advise me on how to behave on the opening day of school. She spoke about the importance of first impressions, good manners and paying attention. I was astonished at how accurately she had internalized all of her parents' clichés. Even the ones during which she had defiantly covered her ears and screamed, "I'm not listening to you!" Word by word, inflection by inflection, she had them all down pat.

We both laughed as she recited the whole *spiel*.

What do you tell your daughter before she goes around the world: Be careful? Don't catch cold? Don't talk to strangers? Don't fall off the pyramids? Be sure to wear your hat?

(Take something with you, made by your grandmother, so mom and I can pretend we can still protect you from all harm?)

But by then, she was already driving away to only God knows where.

Who Is a Rich Man?

ABOUT SIX MONTHS AFTER HIS FIRST HEART ATTACK, Karen suggested that I take my father away overnight—just like he used to take me away on fishing trips when I was a kid. So I found an inn up on Lake St. Clair, an hour north of Detroit, where the two of us—now that we both realized he wasn't going to live forever—could have some time alone. We took the newly completed Reuther Freeway all the way to the end and from there headed north toward Mount Clemens. There used to be some kind of spa there where all the Jews went. There is also a big cemetery where my father's parents are buried. We visited their graves.

After serving in the Navy during World War II, my dad got a job as a display artist and later as an appliance salesman for Sears & Roebuck. After he retired, he spent the last fifteen years of his life as a kind of executive superintendent at the temple where I grew up. I don't think it ever occurred to him to ask for a penny. He just liked helping people. I guess other people liked it, too. Seven hundred people came to his funeral.

We drove on that freeway as if it were a plateau out of time. And then, as if he had been secretly rehearsing it for years, my father said something that still strikes me as a confession of the bittersweet reality of what it means to be a "provider."

"I suppose" he muttered, "I wish I could have earned more money for your mother and you boys. I thought I made all the right decisions at the time, but now, in retrospect, I guess some of them lost us money."

That had never occurred to me. I knew we weren't wealthy like many people we knew, but I always thought we were well off. Sure, while I was growing up I wanted to be able to buy fancier clothes at fancier stores, but we always seemed to have enough money for vacations that seemed fun and exciting. We would drive up into Northern Michigan or take the train to Chicago and stay in the best hotel for a few days. I am astonished, as I look back, that it never once occurred to me or my brother that we should go to the Caribbean or to Europe or that we should own a vacation home or two cars. I think now that if such thoughts had occurred to my father, he had kept them a secret from all of us, maybe even from himself.

Once my father built a patio behind our house. We bought a charcoal grill and my mother gave him a chef's hat and invited my older cousin Marty and his kids over for a barbecue on a perfect Sunday afternoon. As dad set a hamburger from the grill onto a paper plate, he said with a grin, "I wonder what the poor people are doin' today?"

Just a few years before he died, I finally convinced him that he could afford to sell the house, move into a garden apartment and, as they say, live off the interest. We stood there watching the movers position the sofa. He said to me, "Larry, I feel like a rich man."

So when he died a few years later, and my brother and I chose an inscription for his tombstone, we agreed on the Talmudic passage: "Who is rich? He who is content with his portion."

Memory's Price

MY FATHER WAS, AMONG MANY THINGS, a sign painter. I grew up amidst art gum erasers, mat board and paint brushes. So now, every now and then, when I reach out to pick up a roll of masking tape, I bring back more than the tape. Sometimes, for just a moment or two, I cry and I remember how he taught me how to hold a brush.

He was also the first trainer of the Detroit Lions—back in 1935 when they were world champs. Sunday afternoons, while growing up, I would watch their games with him on television. So, even now, when I hear the sportscaster mention the Detroit Lions, without warning, I get sad.

He used to love peaches. They could be in ice cream, or on his cereal, but he especially loved fresh whole peaches. So now, when I drive by a fruit stand selling peaches, every now and then, I imagine that he is with me in the car and how we would pull over and buy a half dozen. And again my eyes moisten.

I have come to regard these unexpected tears as a natural part of the healing process, even as a precious reminder of my love for him. After several years, I am getting used to it, but I hope it never stops.

I feel sometimes almost as if all the things that remind me of my father were joined to me by long, thin, taut wires. And when I chance upon one of those things—the masking tape, the football game, the fresh peaches—one of the wires gets twisted ever so slightly and it pinches out another tear or two I didn't know I had. Even more mysterious to me is that every few weeks, I discover yet another wire. There seem to be thousands of them.

When my mother, my brother and I walked down the aisle just behind the rabbis who were following his casket, I cried openly. The young assistant rabbi looked back in concern to make sure I was all right. I managed to joke, "Six years of psychoanalysis, now I can cry whenever I want."

My father lived to be 76. Not a ripe old age, but long enough to make it to two of the three *b'nai mitzvah* of my kids. Since he succumbed to a heart attack, neither my brother nor I were able to get there in time, as it says in Genesis, to close his eyes. But we were spared the scene of a hospital room and only have memories of his healthy smile. I suppose I was even fortunate that we had him for eight years after his first big heart attack.

He was my father and he's dead. And every now and then, sometimes once a day, other times every week or two, but sooner or later, one of the wires gets twisted and I cry a little. It is a small price to pay for our love. It is almost as if his death has made his life even more precious.

Net Work

Through trees which grow very slowly, silently and when no one is looking, through houses which, if properly maintained, can live for hundreds of years; through rocks and soil which will just lay there forever if left alone; and through movies which often only live for a month or so; through food on the kitchen counter which grows moldy within days; through the tears of a child which can change to laughter in a moment…

Through all this lifestuff, gray hair, the "rearrangement" of our bodily weight, the death of a friend, the wedding of a "mere child," we are occasionally reminded that we are growing old. Moving along with us at precisely the same speed, so that we are not aware of their chronological motion any more than we are aware of our own, are our mothers and fathers, brothers and sisters, husbands and wives, sons and daughters. Everyone else grows old at precisely the same rate that we do. The rate of our "inflation" is indexed to each other so that we often do not realize what is going on.

There we find ourselves, hauled along in the strands of some great net, probably against our will and certainly without our awareness, through trees and houses and soil, through movies and food and crying children. Occasionally, we grab onto something and manage, for a time, to drag it along with us, fixing it, repairing it, insuring it, cleansing it. But sooner or later, we lose our grip on it and it slides out of the net of our relationships.

People go on growing, but the net of relationships which binds them to one another remains constant. A father is always a father, even when he is too old to do what a father has done all his life, and even when he is long dead. A spouse, a sibling, a child will always stand in the same relationship and be hauled through Creation along with you. As surely as your mother says at least once a visit, "No matter what, you'll always be my little boy," or as surely as a younger brother, no matter how diligently he tries, can never catch up on the six-year lead his big sister has on him—the net never changes.

We can't do anything about this great net of the generations. We are simply in it, held in relationship to one another, carried along, with or without our consent, like ornaments on some great invisible tapestry. Every now and then we are given permission to realize our place in its ancient fabric and stand reverent. We meet God in the faces of our parents and in the faces of our children because the very existence of other generations means that we have been born and that we will die.

And yet, as surely as it is difficult to comprehend our place in the net, when we manage for a moment to feel its gentle but inexorable motion, we rise above it like a soaring, lone bird. The cords are transformed into lifelines and we are blessed to glide through all Creation even as the bird is blessed and free to return to its nest.

Liquid Photographs

I READ RECENTLY that the Bettman Photographic Archives had been purchased by the owner of the world's largest software company. Apparently, he intends to digitize the photos and make them available, for a price, to anyone with a computer.

Ironically, transforming them into computer images may deprive them of the very permanence that made them important. Through the amazing technology of photographic manipulation, it is now possible to take any photo and change it in literally *any* imaginable way. Not only can you remove blemishes, you can remove people, you can add people, you can change their expressions, postures, clothes, even their body parts. And when you print the new photographic image, there is no way that anyone can say for sure that the photo has been retouched. Not only do photos now lie, they are just another malleable medium for our wildest imagination. This could save a lot of families from needless pain.

On the inside book flap of the first edition of my first book is a photo of the author which his young wife took. It was conceived and cropped to make the author resemble as much as possible the most venerated sage of the past generation of Jews, Abraham Joshua Heschel. Since in those days I had a lot more hair on my head and a much longer beard, this wasn't as preposterous as it might sound. In fact, when I first grew my beard in graduate school, a classmate quipped that I looked just like Heschel when he was three.

My publisher took it into his head that a fifteenth anniversary edition of the book needed a new photo of the author. That wasn't a problem. The problem was that he wanted to print the first photo along with it.

"You mean," I said with a wince, "sort of like a 'before and after' shot for a men's hair loss program."

"No," he explained. "I want our generation to realize that a lot can change in fifteen years. I think it will help people get a sense of perspective on the book and on themselves."

When he talks like that, there's no arguing with him.

All of this is a roundabout way to get you into our basement which is where my wife and I wound up looking for the originals of the photos. We were in the cellar because I am in charge of the family albums in our house. I go through each roll of film and pick out the half dozen best shots. The rest I throw away. That's what history's all about: Saving photos of yourself that make you look good.

When we were first married, my wife saw me tossing away these photographic rejects.

"What are you doing?" she gasped.

"I'm throwing away these photographs you said you hated."

"Oh no you're not. They're staying right here."

"But in a few years there will be huge boxes filled with them."

"I don't care. They don't leave the house."

And sure enough, now almost two decades later, they were still there in cardboard boxes in the cellar. And here we were at 11:30 at night trying to find one of them.

This was harder than we had imagined because apparently burglars had snuck into the house and dumped all the neatly arranged envelopes with all the negatives and all the slides and all of the prints helter-skelter into random boxes. (It may also have been the children.) Here we were like archaeologists in our own basement, looking at all the pictures of the people we had been pretending we weren't. And, even more unsettling, all the children we had been pretending our children weren't, either. But photos don't lie (at least they didn't until a few years ago) and there we were, not quite as flawless as we were in the family albums up in the living room. No mistaking it: That was *us*.

ALL THIS TIME, I had been pretending that the people in my family looked the way they did in the carefully censored photos in the album. Now I realized that these only captured one moment of millions. And that at each one of those other moments, there were other expressions, other faces, other fears and other dreams, parallel universes. I felt as if we were meeting people we had long ago forgotten. The babies who weren't smiling, the little girl who was blinking as the photo was taken, this little boy with a tearful pout, that one slightly out of focus.

"See," she smiled, "he looks just like your father in this one…"

At the time it was taken we were unable to see it, but now, through the prism of the years, it was unmistakable. We wrench an image out of time, freeze it, hold it up to the light and marvel. We even delude ourselves into thinking that it captures the incessant motion of life.

At any given moment, of course, we all look like something. But by the next, we're already on our way to becoming someone else. Maybe that's why at Mount Sinai God says, "You can't make an image of Me. It's not that I'm invisible, I just don't look like anything. There's nothing to see. How else would you expect Me to be in every family photo?"

3. RESPONSIBILITY

Stranger on the Bus

A LIGHT SNOW WAS FALLING and the streets were crowded with people. It was Munich in Nazi Germany. One of my rabbinic students, Shifra Penzias, told me her great-aunt, Sussie, had been riding a city bus home from work when SS storm troopers suddenly stopped the coach and began examining the identification papers of the passengers. Most were annoyed but a few were terrified. Jews were being told to leave the bus and get into a truck around the corner.

My student's great-aunt watched from her seat in the rear as the soldiers systematically worked their way down the aisle. She began to tremble, tears streaming down her face. When the man next to her noticed that she was crying, he politely asked her why.

"I don't have the papers you have. I am a Jew. They're going to take me."

The man exploded with disgust. He began to curse and scream at her. "You stupid bitch," he roared. "I can't stand being near you!"

The SS men asked what all the yelling was about.

"Damn her," the man shouted angrily. "My wife has forgotten her papers again! I'm so fed up. She always does this!"

The soldiers laughed and moved on.

My student said that her great-aunt never saw the man again. She never even knew his name.

YOU ARE GOING ABOUT YOUR BUSINESS when you stumble onto something that has your name on it. Or, to be more accurate, a task with your name on it finds you. Its execution requires inconvenience, self-sacrifice, even risk. You step forward and encounter your destiny. This does not mean you must do everything that lands on your doorstep, or that you should assume every risk or make every self-sacrifice. But it does mean that you must tell yourself the truth about where you have been placed and why.

You do not exercise your freedom by doing what you want. Self-indulgence is not an exercise of freedom. But when you accept the task that destiny seems to have set before you, you become free. Perhaps the only exercise of real freedom comes from doing what you were meant to do all along.

If everything is connected to everything else, then everyone is ultimately responsible for everything. We can blame *nothing* on anyone else. The more we comprehend our mutual interdependence, the more we fathom the implications of our most trivial acts. We find ourselves within a luminous organism of sacred responsibility.

Even on a bus in Munich.

Ability to Respond

IN THE FILM VERSION of Tom Clancy's novel *Clear and Present Danger*, Harrison Ford plays the acting director of the C. I. A. He is caught and nearly murdered in a secret war between the President of the United States and the Colombian drug cartel. His enemies are convinced there are only shades of moral gray and that Ford is just a "boy scout." But Ford believes that you can know the difference between right and wrong—and that you must act accordingly.

After realizing he's been set up, Ford and a friend go into the Colombian jungle searching for survivors of an American commando team. Even though their existence, betrayal and almost total destruction have been concealed from him, Ford feels morally bound to try to save whomever he can. Only one survivor remains hidden in the mountains. Enraged, the commando screams, "Who did this to us? Who is responsible?" But before either of his rescuers can explain the Byzantine plots of their puppet masters, Ford steps forward and, to the stunned silence of his partner and the commando, he utters the words, "I am."

"*I am responsible.*"

WHAT MAKES THIS LINE SO POWERFUL is that we know he was *not* responsible. Indeed, *he* is a victim of the same machinery as the commando. Yet, now he is risking his life to take responsibility for what has happened, to try to fix what others have done.

We are unaccustomed to such heroism. What makes Ford's character so remarkable is that the boundaries of his sense of obligation extend beyond his own self-interest. This man is simply doing what needs to be done. He says, in effect, "Well, if anyone is responsible, it must be me. The wicked men who set this up will have books filled with excuses. They'll get off with slaps on the wrist and die in their sleep. No, the one who is responsible is the one who is present now in this place."

I am fascinated that the word "responsible" has two different meanings. One connotes guilt, blame and punishment, as in, "Who's *responsible* for this mess?"; the other seems focused on the present and connotes moral maturity, as in, "She is a very *responsible* woman." The former means, "blame"; the latter draws its meaning from "able to respond," that is, "response-able." Thus, one who is guilty, but denies it, is not *able to respond*. And conversely, one who is *not* guilty nevertheless might still be responsible. Every day, situations arise which require the action of a responsible person.

My son recently told me that being an unemployed screen writer is not nearly as bad as being an unemployed actor.

"They're both just different forms of artistic expression," I said.

"No," he taught me, "if they don't buy your writing, they reject your work. But if they don't buy your acting, they reject you."

You are how you act, how you act toward the people you meet. You extend no farther than the outer perimeter of your responsibility.

Breaking Chandeliers

WE HAVE LIVED IN THE SAME HOUSE for almost a quarter of a century. The house was built the same year that I was: 1943. Keeping it in good shape, therefore, has some symbolic, personal significance.

Like all young couples moving into their first and, in our case, only home, we naturally developed a long list of modifications, improvements, repairs—a wish list. Over the years, new items get added to take the place of those finally completed or of those demoted in importance as our tastes and needs changed. Always, near the bottom of the list, was the chandelier in the dining room. It wasn't broken nor did it look particularly awful. We just didn't like it very much. It became a sort of family joke. Friends would tease, "You still have that ugly chandelier in the dining room?" It wasn't egregiously wrong enough to require immediate attention, so, as with so many things in life, whenever we found some money or energy, we wound up spending them on something else. Rooms were painted and wallpapered. Floors were sanded and varnished. The roof was replaced. We even put on an addition. But the chandelier remained.

Then, one afternoon during my parents' semiannual visit from Detroit, my father showed up in the dining room with a hammer.

"What's that for?" I asked.

"I was gonna break that chandelier you're always complaining about," he said. "I figured if somebody didn't break it, you'd never get around to getting yourselves a new one."

That's the lesson he taught me: Some things you just have to break or they'll stay there forever. So, together, my Dad and I got the stepladder from the basement and took down the chandelier, leaving only bare light bulbs. Now something *had* to be done. The next day we went to the lamp store and bought a new one.

IT IS A CURIOUS BUT LITTLE KNOWN FACT that the Israelites enslaved in Egypt for four hundred years never once asked to go free. Nowhere in the Hebrew Bible do they say to Pharaoh or Moses or God, "Get us out of here!" All they say, and they say it a lot and in a lot of different ways, is: Life is hard; we don't like it.

This may explain why God had to put on such a big show with all those miracles and plagues. If God had simply wanted them free, God could have just made them free. But that wouldn't have been enough. The slaves themselves had to *want* to go free. Only by watching all those great signs and portents might they, little by little, begin to realize *for themselves* that there was a power in the universe even greater than Pharaoh, a power dedicated to freeing slaves.

What had to be "broken" was not Pharaoh's will, but the dullness of their own routine, the comfortable reliability of putting up with things the way they were.

ACCORDING TO KUSHNER FAMILY LEGEND, the reason my grandparents left their village in the Ukraine was on account of a chandelier that had been one of my grandfather's most prized possessions.

My Aunt Lena, who was sixteen at the time, told me just before she died thirty years ago that whenever it looked like there might be trouble with the local peasants, my grandfather would first shepherd the family to safety in the root cellar, then carefully take the chandelier down so it wouldn't get damaged by rocks or beets thrown through the windows.

"On Friday nights," she said, "they'd come home from the fields and make trouble."

"Was it a pogrom?" I asked.

"No, just the local peasants," she said. "And one week, while Pa was trying to get that chandelier safely into the attic, he dropped it and it broke with a crash into a thousand pieces. I overheard him say to Ma, 'That does it: We're going to America.'"

Seamonds

THE FIRST TIME I SAW MY FATHER I was two and a half years old. We met at Michigan Central Depot in Detroit. He had come on the train from Great Lakes Naval Base in Illinois. The navy had sent him to Australia during the war in the Pacific just three months before I was born. I have looked through the photos and some of the correspondence trying to understand what this separation must have been like for my parents.

My dad worked his way up to the rank of Chief Petty Officer. He had a formal studio photograph taken for my mother showing him in his uniform with his left arm turned in ever so slightly so that it revealed the three red V's with the red arch over the white eagle and the red cross which meant he was now a Chief Pharmacist's Mate.

The base where he was stationed in Sydney didn't have a synagogue, so my father found a nearby civilian congregation where he attended services. He was not an especially religious Jew, more likely just a serviceman looking for a place that reminded him of home.

A prominent member of the congregation, Immanuel Seamonds, saw this lone American sailor and invited my father to sit with him and his family. Over the months, a friendship developed. When Seamonds learned that I had been born, he scoured the city of Sydney to find another Jewish family that had a boy born on September 22, my birthday. And from that day on, my father and this family with the little baby boy were invited to the Seamonds' home every Sabbath afternoon so that my father shouldn't get cheated out of watching his son grow up.

THE OTHER DAY, while looking through a batch of postcards that I had collected as a boy—some I had bought myself, but most I had inherited from my grandmother—I was surprised to find one I had never noticed before. It was not a commercially mass-produced card. It was the same size and weight of such a card, but was obviously a photo that had been printed so that it could be mailed as a postcard, a one-of-a-kind item. It was addressed to my mother and bore the mark of the United States Naval Censor. There were three people in it. In the middle was my father, wearing his navy uniform. I could date it at once from the number of stripes on his sleeve and from the way he had trimmed his mustache. It was 1944, maybe six months after I had been born. He had his arms around a man and a woman. They were both smiling. I am certain that it was Immanuel and Rose Seamonds.

This is how I met Immanuel Seamonds for the first time, in a batch of postcards in the bottom of a drawer.

Jury Duty

TELLING THEM YOU'RE A RABBI will not get you out of jury duty in the Commonwealth of Massachusetts. As far as I can tell from the bizarre excuses that my fellow jurors tried on the authorities, *nothing* will get you out of jury duty. Like them, until I wound up on a jury for a three-day, criminal trial a few years ago, my knowledge of the judicial process was a sophisticated quilt pieced together of fragments from "L. A. Law," "Perry Mason" and "Wapner's Court."

The process of reaching any verdict—the very etymology of the word means, "speak the truth" (as if it were a request for how many potatoes are in the sack)—and then the awesomeness of saying to another human being, "You are innocent" or "You are guilty," is more ambiguous, less satisfying and more disturbing than anything television had led me to believe.

"The defendant has chosen his constitutional right to have his case adjudicated by the people of the United States and *you*," said the judge, looking solemnly right at us, "are they."

It worked. Her words cut through hours of hoping I wouldn't get called or that I would be disqualified so that I could get back to my life's routine. Her words struck me with such power that I didn't even have time to feel ashamed.

The defendant had been indicted for trafficking in cocaine. Not once during the three-day trial did he utter so much as one word. We never once heard the sound of the voice of the man over whom we sat in judgment. From the way he looked, it is unlikely that his vocabulary or voice could do anything but further damage his shaky case. Even in the white shirt and the same tie he wore throughout the entire trial, he looked like a low-life, a pusher, a dirtball. One of my fellow jurors jokingly whispered to me after the first day of the trial, "Fry the sucker."

Fourteen of us were on the panel. Since we were instructed not to discuss the evidence or the trial until it was completed and were frequently sequestered in the jury room with nothing but jelly donuts and bad coffee, we were condemned to small talk and trying to figure out as much as we could about one another without seeming nosy. There was a dental hygienist whom I conjectured had tried her share of coke, a high school guidance counselor, an art dealer, a convenience store proprietor who may have done some minor league trafficking himself, a businessman and a software engineer.

There was even an honest-to-goodness, semiretired farmer who inadvertently entertained us urban and suburban snobs with stories about milking cows and dressing turkeys. He wore low-fashion blue jeans and a red plaid work shirt and carried a few sheets of paper towel in his back pocket which he used as a handkerchief.

RABBI ZALMAN SCHACHTER-SHALOMI, a founder of the contemporary Jewish renewal movement, used to tell about a fellow who heard that Sabbath in the town of Libush, when its rabbi was still alive, was like Sabbath in Paradise: Beautiful, joyous, peaceful beyond description. Determined to find the secret of its beauty, he returned, at great expense, to the town. But no one knew the secret because they had not yet been born or were too old to remember Sabbath in the days of the great rabbi. The traveler finally found an old washer-woman who had worked in the kitchen when the rabbi lived.

"So what was the secret of the Sabbath day that made it like the Messiah's time? What exactly did the rabbi do that made it so sweet?"

"Oh, I was just a girl," she demurred. "I remember that in the kitchen before *Shabbos* there was a lot of commotion. Important guests were arriving from far and wide. Everything had to be just so. We were all under a great deal of pressure. In the tumult, we would bump into one another, step on one another's toes. Sometimes we would even yell at one another."

"Yes," said the traveler, "but what was so *special* about *Shabbos*?"

"I only remember we would get very angry with one another. Oh yes, and every week we would always forget."

"Forget what?"

"The Rebbe would walk in, and in the most kindly voice he would ask us if we remembered. But from one week to the next we always forgot."

"Forgot *what*?"

"We always forgot to forgive one another. And as soon as we remembered to forgive one another, it was *Shabbos*. Just like that."

EACH TIME WE WERE SUMMONED into the courtroom, the bailiff lined us up single file in our assigned places and we waited. Leaning in the corner next to the door of the jury room was a long, white pole, similar to the handle of a push broom, each end painted tan. "What's that?" asked the housewife in front of me. Having no clue at all, I suggested we could use it to play limbo if things got boring.

We heard days of testimony and examined over twenty pieces of evidence. We learned from experts about the medical and psychological effects of cocaine addiction, the intricacies of how to manufacture crack from cocaine and the laws of Massachusetts defining "trafficking," which, I imagine to the dismay of the defense, include simply "giving" the proscribed substance to another person.

At the conclusion of her charge to the jury, the judge announced that juror Number 10, Lawrence Kushner, would be the foreman. Since both the prosecution and defense had access to my juror information card upon which I had dutifully filled in my occupation, I figured that they both thought they were giving themselves a break: One figured that clergy would be hard on morals, the other that I would be a bleeding heart softy. We marched single file back to the jury room. The bailiff explained that he would now take the long white limbo pole and wedge it against the door, literally locking us into our deliberation.

Having a legal system at the core of our religious culture, Jews take judgment very seriously. On every rabbinic certificate of ordination, it says in Hebrew: *Yoreh yoreh*, "this one is fit to teach;" *yadin yadin*, "this one is fit to judge." On the other hand, we are equally bullish on forgiveness. We have no concept of three strikes and you're out. Seeking and receiving forgiveness is ever possible, even unto the moment of death.

The Talmud counsels us with a spate of judicial aphorisms: Never "judge alone, for only God can do that. . . ."

"Judge all people in the scale of merit," which means that we must give others the benefit of the doubt. And, as if these left any question, "Do not judge your neighbor until you have stood in his place." It occurs to me that this may effectively mean you can never judge anyone.

The defendant was not what you would call a big-time pusher, just an addict whose life was a dead end. The police raided the pig sty where he lived hoping to make a big drug bust. But there was no crack-making machinery, no lists of names, no stash of drugs, no bags of money. Just the defendant and a friend, wrecked out of their minds. Beneath one of the cushions where they were sitting was a bag with 15 grams of coke. The defendant had thirty-one cents. Was he guilty of "trafficking"? Probably, but I'm not convinced. Along with a few other jurors, I suspected the police were also trying to salvage an expensive, failed stakeout.

After several hours, we were still split. And I got to worrying that the jury was on trial, too. I became increasingly convinced that the defendant might be innocent of trafficking. Five of us remained unswayed by the evidence "beyond a reasonable doubt." This was the hardest discussion group I'd ever led. Finally all those years of Talmud paid off: "Look," I proposed to my fellow jurors, "not all giving is *giving*. If, as you're leaving my house I say, 'Here, I'd like you to have this bottle of expensive Scotch, take it home, it's yours,' that means I gave it to you. But if during a visit, I offer you a shot of whiskey and you accept, I didn't give it to you. I *shared* it with you."

I rang the bell for the bailiff. He unlocked the door and solemnly led us into the courtroom. I handed the bailiff the verdict sheet on which I had carefully marked our decision.

"How say you members of the jury? Guilty or Not guilty?"

(I was shaking.)

"We find the defendant guilty of the lesser charge of possession, but *not* guilty of trafficking."

There were a few gasps. Some people in the gallery hugged one another. I was overwhelmed by the power of the ritual, by our power over this man's life, over the simple gesture of judging another human being and finding him innocent.

As we marched single file back into the jury room, the bailiff whispered under his breath, "Good verdict." The judge joined us to add her gratitude for our work and for our decision. "He's been clean now since his arrest so I sentenced him to the sixty days time he's already served. I didn't want to have to put him in jail and all the rehabilitation programs already have long waiting lists."

TO BE FORGIVEN, YOU MUST FIRST LEARN HOW TO FORGIVE. Many of us waste years waiting to be forgiven. But since we have never offered forgiveness ourselves, we do not know how to recognize it when it is extended to us. To "forgive" means not only to excuse someone for having committed an offense, but also to renounce anger and claims of resentment. Forgiving someone therefore means you are willing to endure the risk that he will hurt you in exactly the same way again, but that you trust him not to.

THE JURY WAS DISCHARGED. As we walked down the corridor, our footsteps echoing on the marble floor, we turned the corner and there, at the other end of the hall, by a second bank of elevators, we saw the public defender standing with the defendant and his mother. We smiled. "Thank you," called the public defender.

And then something got into me. I broke ranks and walked the few dozen steps toward the defendant. They seemed like a football field. After all, I was the foreman and though no one here but the defense attorney knew it, I was also a rabbi. But at this particular moment, I also felt like a person who had been given an opportunity to say one thing. It could not be a conversation nor a paragraph. I rehearsed the words in my mind as I walked. When we were face-to-face, I said it: "Very few human beings are offered a real opportunity for a second chance. I hope you will not waste what we have tried to give you."

Then I realized, to my surprise, that I was not alone. Standing behind me is another juror. He, too, felt compelled to speak: "I'm really prayin' for ya, buddy." It was the farmer. As the two of us turned and walked back to the other members of the jury waiting for the elevator, I noticed that the farmer's face was red and streaming with tears. He said to me, choking back a cry, "That guy, that dirtball, he coulda' been my brother."

Someone pressed "Lobby" and we hurried to our cars, hoping to beat rush hour traffic.

Field of Dreams

A FEW YEARS AGO, OUR TEMPLE ADMINISTRATOR TOLD ME I should see a new film called *Field of Dreams*.

"It is a spiritual movie," she said. "It's about impossible things that remind you of something else. It makes you feel better about life."

Since I try to never miss a chance to feel better about life, I took her advice.

Essentially, the film is about an Iowa farmer who keeps hearing a voice that says, "If you build it, he will come," only to learn that the "it" refers to a baseball stadium in the middle of his farm and the "he" refers to "Shoeless Joe" Jackson and other long-dead members of the Chicago White Sox accused of throwing the 1919 World Series. It is also about how the farmer resolves his differences with his estranged (and also long-dead) father with whom he used to play catch.

The farmer does what the voice says and sure enough, from the standing corn just beyond right field, people who many years ago had left this life with unfinished business come walking out and finish the game.

Don't get me wrong. I may write books with the word "spiritual" in the subtitles, but I don't really believe such things are possible. A pillar of cloud or fire? The sun standing still? The Red Sea splitting? Piece of cake. But resurrected members of a baseball team? No way.

And yet, I bought it. I left the theater with the mischievous, reassuring hunch that such things were possible. That may be why the film was so gratifying.

YEHUDA ARYEH LEIB OF GER, a nineteenth century Hasidic master, taught that "through the power of performing a religious act, some spiritual power is awakened. And so it is with everything a person does." In other words, we can only light the matches, but we cannot keep them burning. We can kindle a match, but we cannot sustain a fire. For we have no real power of our own. We have only the capacity to initiate light. The rest is up to God.

Anything accomplished by the power of a human being sooner or later must stop. But when the power of the Holy One is awakened, this kind of power continues forever. The whole idea behind performing religious deeds is to set things in their proper places until they are joined to their source. In the language of the Kabbalistic maxim: "By means of the awakening below, comes the awakening on high."

WHAT *FIELD OF DREAMS* SAID was that by doing what you believe you must do, you can sometimes awaken something in another universe and rouse a power far beyond anything you could ever hope to understand. At the end of the film, the eye of the camera slowly moved higher and panned out into the evening distance to reveal thousands of headlights silently winding their way toward the grandstand in the corn field. The message for me was that there are a lot of people driving around out there looking for someone who listens to "the voice" and is willing to do something about it, even if it doesn't make sound business sense.

You cannot force the hand of that kind of power. But through quiet, usually faltering, but faithful diligence, you can awaken it in yourself, in your long-dead parents, and maybe even in the players on the 1919 Chicago White Sox.

Single Handing

SAILING A BIG BOAT IS ONE THING; sailing it alone is something else. There is no one who can help you, no one you can ask. You must be prepared to fix—or live with—every contingency. Worse than being at the mercy of the elements, you are at the mercy of yourself and whatever you cannot handle alone. No matter how carefully you think through the sail in advance, no matter how many backup systems you have arranged, inevitably, something will go wrong that requires immediate correction. You are then alone with your own ingenuity, fortitude, courage. What goes wrong could come from the sea, the wind, your own stupidity, the boat, the equipment, the sails. And it usually makes something else go wrong. And you are alone.

I was surprised, therefore, when a friend who's a licensed Coast Guard captain suggested, "Being a single hander is easy."

"Sure," I said, "maybe for you. But for those of us who are beginners, no way."

"Wrong," he teased, "it's really easy. All you have to do is walk forward to the bow, stoop down to where the mooring line is made fast to the cleat, untie that line and drop it in the water. Presto, you're a single hander!"

"What do you mean?" I asked.

"You can pick it up again immediately—you had a short sail. Or you can sail around the world before you come back to the mooring again.

"We're not talking about *whether or not* you have the nerve to single hand the boat. We're only talking about how long. Short sail, long sail, it doesn't matter. Either way, you're a single hander."

Moving along by the grace of a power we cannot see. Neither of the earth nor of the sky. Hovering between them. Belonging to neither. Going forth by yourself.

MY FRIEND'S ADVICE REMINDED ME OF AN OLD LEGEND about crossing the Red Sea. According to tradition, the waters did not split until one man, Nahshon ben Aminidab, walked into them up to his nostrils. God then said, "For *him*, I will split the sea."

The redemption, the miracle, the transformation, they are all in *your* hands. Or, more precisely, in letting go of whatever you are holding. You let go of the line and set forward into the sea. How else would you expect the voyage to begin?

Hershey with Almonds

WHEN KAREN WAS PREGNANT WITH OUR SECOND CHILD, we lived in a little shoebox of an apartment in the town of Marlborough outside of Boston. In the dead of winter and the middle of the night, she awakened me with a confession.

"Larry, I know this sounds crazy, but I would give anything for a chocolate bar, especially one with almonds."

I knew at once that this was the mythic "strange craving" of a pregnant woman. Before she could even call it a request, I jumped out of bed, pulled my Levi's on over my pajamas, a sweatshirt, then my snow parka, boots, hat, gloves.

"Don't worry about a thing, sweetheart," I said. (After all, she'd been carrying our child around in her belly now for six months. This was the least I could do.)

When I got downstairs, I realized that it had been snowing for a few hours. The car was covered with a few inches of heavy, wet slush. But only after I had managed to clean it off did it dawn on me: Where would I find a chocolate bar in Marlborough, Massachusetts, in the middle of the night, in a blizzard? And then it hit me: Of course, at the Holiday Inn out on I-495.

The night clerk watched incredulously as a man in pajamas and snow parka skidded to a stop under the portico, ran inside, punched quarters into the candy machine, waved and drove off into the snowstorm.

I presented my offering. Karen was a little embarrassed, but unequivocally grateful. As for me, I learned something precious about myself. I normally have a well developed ego, but for about forty-five minutes twenty years ago, I did not have an ego of my own. Instead, I was only an extension of Karen Kushner's ego. Instead of doing what I wanted and remaining in a warm bed, I did what she wanted and drove around in the middle of the night in a blizzard looking for a chocolate bar.

And here's the amazing part. It made me happier to do what my wife wanted than to do what I wanted. By letting go of my ego, I was happier than if I had tried to please myself. By doing what your lover wants, you transcend yourself. So it is with all sacred deeds. We give ourselves over to them, humbly offer ourselves as servants of something or someone greater. In so doing, we are transformed.

The Roofer

WHEN I WAS JUST OUT OF RABBINIC SCHOOL, I accepted a fellowship at a wealthy congregation in one of Chicago's North Shore suburbs. It was a good place, rich not only in money, but in such things as creativity, learning and, especially, political activism. The main prayer hall, already dramatic with its high, modern, great, white walls and ceiling, frequently witnessed controversy, radical orators, even guerrilla theater.

In such a place, especially in the early 1970s, religious study often naturally focused on the Hebrew prophets and their demand for social justice. These few dozen divinely commissioned biblical teachers, who claimed their mouths had been taken over by God, forever changed the scope of religious history. No one knows why, in the middle of the eighth pre-Christian century, they burst on the scene. Or why, three hundred years later, their voices were stilled. Because their message was so strident and their warning so dreadful, they were derided and ridiculed when they were not being ignored. Yet two millennia later, no serious student of Western religious history can summarily dismiss even an obviously schizophrenic, street-corner prophet: He just might be speaking for God. One rule of thumb is that if you like the message, the prophet's probably a fake; but if he makes you uncomfortable, then listen up.

Almost everyone on the North Shore who worked downtown in Chicago commuted there via the Chicago &

Northwestern Railroad. Each morning, the long, double-decker, green and yellow trains streamed into C.N. & W. Station, emptying the suburbs, filling the Loop. Waves of people with attaché cases and newspapers scurried through the terminal. Such crowds are irresistible magnets for people selling just about everything, even social justice. And sure enough, there, in one of the long corridors, a tall, intense, bearded, wild-eyed man, calling himself, "Eliezer, Servant of the Lord," had taken up his position, admonishing anyone willing to listen. A roofer by occupation, Eliezer's message was hardly novel, little more than warmed-over Deuteronomic theory of history, the sort of cosmic bogey-man stuff that liberals are quick to dismiss: "You've been bad, so the house is coming down! Etcetera. Etcetera."

And, just as with true (and would-be) prophets throughout history, the busy commuters ignored him—except for a few members of our congregation, who had been studying the Hebrew Bible. They knew that you are supposed to stop and pay the man some attention. And when they did, to their discomfort, they found that his message was neither inappropriate nor crazy. Disconcerting, unimaginative, unsettling, yes. But not crazy.

Soon, a few congregants decided to speak with the rabbi of the congregation. Without hesitation, he agreed to invite Eliezer, "Servant of the Lord," roofer (and possibly prophet) to preach at services in the big white prayer hall in the suburbs.

Eliezer drew a good sized crowd, bigger than many pundits with more credentials had drawn at the same synagogue. It was a spring evening with a light drizzle. Folks listened politely, even as their boredom gave way to disappointment with the predictability of his message. Then, fifteen minutes into the jeremiad, there was a loud clap of thunder and a few people gasped as a thin crack appeared in the middle of the high white ceiling. Drops of rain water began dripping into the sanctuary. The people who were getting wet moved to drier seats. Eliezer finished his sermon. Monday morning, they called the contractor. Years later, I heard that "Eliezer, Servant of the Lord" had emigrated to Israel where he wound up in jail for being a public nuisance.

Reciting Psalms

AT A SUMMER INSTITUTE WHERE I WAS TEACHING a class on the meaning of sacred text, we studied a Hasidic story which taught that the text not only described, but actually contained the event itself. If read properly, the event could be summoned and relived. This reminded one student, Milt Zaiment, of something he had done as a boy more than sixty years before when his uncle had pneumonia.

"In those days, people didn't go to hospitals like they do now. My uncle lay in his bedroom and the doctor, a good man, came out and told my parents that the end was near. 'I'm sorry,' he consoled, 'but I don't expect him to live through the night.' We helped the doctor on with his coat and saw him to the door.

'Come,' said my father, taking me by the hand. 'We have a job to do.' He sat me down next to my uncle's bed, sat next to me, opened the Bible and recited a Psalm. Then he gave the book to me. 'Now you read.' When I finished, he took the book from me and read the next Psalm. And so it went, all through the night, the two of us reciting Psalms, one after another.

When morning came, my uncle was still alive. The doctor returned. He was amazed. He said he had never seen anything like it, that it was a miracle. My father smiled respectfully. He washed his face, had a cup of coffee and went to work. He never said a word about that night. My uncle lived another forty years."

4. CONNECTION

Trout Fishing

A MEMBER OF MY CONGREGATION TOLD ME that he had gone to his rabbi with a confession the week before his bar mitzvah: He didn't think he could go through with the ceremony because he didn't believe in God. The rabbi thought for a moment and then asked kindly, "What makes you think it matters to God?"

You don't have to believe in psychoanalysis to have an unconscious, either. Therapy just helps you discover how often this hidden dimension of your psyche influences your life. Something else is going on beneath the surface. Think of analysis as a kind of self-discipline that gradually weans you away from blaming so much on chance and gets you to acknowledge your own participation in your life's unfolding. Whereas once you would have thought you misplaced your car keys, "accidentally" preventing you from making an unpleasant trip, now you realize that it wasn't a coincidence at all. The whole business was the result of a "deliberate," though unconscious, wish. In this way, you learn to take ever increasing measures of responsibility for how your life is turning out. There's more to reality than meets the eye and more forces at work that we cannot ordinarily see which exert profound influences on us. Surely no one could know them all.

My own calendar is hopelessly complicated. Between teaching in Manhattan, lecturing in distant cities and tending to the needs of a very active congregation, I consider myself lucky to find an afternoon off every few weeks. Nevertheless, I convinced my eighty-one-year-old, widowed mother to buy a new car, then "allowed" her, at the eleventh hour, to persuade me to fly to Detroit for a day and a half to help her close the deal. After all, she has never bought a car alone. I felt virtuous, even devoted. I told Karen that my dad would want me to do this.

But not until I was on the plane did I realize that my visit came just a few days before the fifth anniversary of my father's death. Suddenly, it was clear: I had unconsciously engineered the whole thing so I could be with my mother, "back in the land of my birth" during these days of memorial. The next day, she and I sat over breakfast at the delicatessen and marveled over the "coincidence" which had brought us together. But I knew better. I had been "arranging" this trip for months.

THE FOLLOWING WEEKEND, Karen went to Florida to visit her parents and I was home alone with our youngest son, Lev. Between the school play, his busy social and athletic schedule and my own work, it is rare that we have such a window together. "Let's rent a movie," I said, "and just hang out."

Lev had sprained his ankle twice recently and this reminded me of the movie *Chariots of Fire*, which I'd been wanting him to see. The film is about two young British runners, one a Scot and the other a Jew, and their paths to the 1924 Olympic games. The opening scene shows the track team running along through the moist sand of a beach on a gray English morning. Lev and I were struck at once by their uniforms and shoes. Compared to today's high-tech athletic equipment, they seemed primitive. I then surprised both of us with an observation: "That's the way it was when Boompa used to train the Detroit Lions football team back in 1935."

I choked back a cry; my eyes filled with tears: This was the anniversary of his death. It was not an accident I chose this movie for this afternoon. My boy put his hand around my shoulder and gave me a hug. "Yeah," he consoled, "those were the days."

In addition to being a sports trainer, my father was also a trout fisherman. As a boy of eight, I rode with him up into northern Michigan to the little town of Lewiston where we "men" would rent a one-room cabin and fish for the weekend. It was 222 miles from home, the longest ride I had ever taken. He taught me how to rub the unassembled ends of the fishing rod in my hair to lubricate them before putting them together and how to "hide" the bottles of Coca-Cola beneath some rocks in the fast running trout stream to keep them cold. And I remember how once, when he caught three fish and I only caught one, he saw the disappointment in my young eyes. So he dropped one of his fish flapping slippery on the grass and said that whoever caught it first could claim to my mother that he had caught it fair and square.

But most of all, I remember the sunlight flooding through the pine trees and the water rushing through the tall grasses and watching him fish downstream.

That evening, some friends asked me to join them for a movie in the city. I was grateful for the company. But when we arrived at the theater we were informed that the print of the film we wanted to see had broken and the eight o'clock show had been canceled. After driving all this way and paying for parking, we were not about to go home without complaint. The manager turned out to be reasonable. Eight of the twelve other films in the complex were already sold out; two others had long lines. So that is how we came to accept complimentary admission to *A River Runs Through It*, a beautifully photographed story based on a memoir by Norman Maclean about his growing up in Montana and trout fishing with his brother and his father, a Presbyterian minister. One of the last lines said something like, "All things flow together into one great unity; and a river runs through it."

Look, I understand about coincidence and even what Jungians call synchronicity. But suppose there is something going on in the universe which is to ordinary, everyday reality as our unconscious is to our daily lives? Softly, but unmistakably guiding it. Pushing us here, pulling us there, tripping us up, guiding our steps, feeding us our lines. Most of the time, we are unaware of it. Yet every now and then, on account of some apparent "fluke," we are startled by the results of its presence, chastened by the forces it exerts on our own secret premeditations. We realize that we have been part of something with neither our consciousness nor consent. It is so sweet—and then it is gone.

You may say, "But I don't believe in God." And I respectfully ask, "What makes you think it matters to God?"

Crime and Punishment

SOMETIMES YOU THINK A STORY IS COMPLETED and all wrapped up. But then, decades later, something happens and you realize that it's not done yet, it's still in process. Take my arrest, for example.

It was the spring of 1972. The war in Vietnam was, as they said, "escalating." Nixon had mined Haiphong Harbor. It was clear that writing a letter to your congressmen was not going to end the horror. Each evening brought new television footage of destruction, carnage, maimed bodies. I began to worry that someday in the distant future I'd bump into some Vietnamese on the street who would ask me what I had been doing when his parents had been napalmed. I decided I wanted to do more than preach sermons. I just didn't know what. The answer came at a routine meeting of the Massachusetts Board of Rabbis.

A group of Jewish college students came to the meeting to ask for our rabbinic participation in an anti-war protest they were planning in front of the Kennedy Federal Building in Boston. In addition to giving their demonstration credibility, they hoped our presence might also keep things safe and under control.

By this time in the war, this was no idle request. Demonstrators had been seriously injured, some had been killed.

Six rabbis volunteered. I was one of them.

THAT FRIDAY EVENING during my sermon, I announced to my congregation that the following week I intended to get arrested in a nonviolent, anti-war demonstration. To my relief, the congregation was solidly behind me. Some members even came downtown to join the crowds of onlookers and lend moral support.

As planned, we all sat down in the big plaza in front of the building and sang Hebrew peace songs. Our crime was to be "blocking an entrance." But after a hour, not a policeman was to be found. Then it dawned on us: They didn't *want* to arrest us. The last thing the government needed was yet another group of religious martyrs being led off to the slammer on the 6 o'clock news.

Finally, a colleague leaned over and said, "Kushner, I know it's not what we planned, but if we want to get arrested, we're gonna have to go inside that building."

So six rabbis and several dozen students got up and began walking through the glass revolving door. And wham! Then it happened. And it happened real fast. No sooner had we entered, than TV cameras and police were everywhere. There was screaming and people were running and falling. We were no longer in control of what was going on. (I remember thinking: "I just hope I don't get hurt.") Out of the corner of my eye, I watched police scuffle some students onto the floor. One policeman nabbed me and a rabbinic colleague with *one* hand.

"Come with me," he said.

We answered, with relief, "We will go peacefully."

The officer took us to the back corner of the lobby where there was this big, waiting freight elevator. We were placed in the custody of a short, ugly man with a badly pockmarked face. He was wearing a black leather coat and deliberately moved his right hand along his waist, pulling back the lapel of his jacket to reveal a pistol holstered on his belt. He said: "You are under arrest."

Then he unsnapped the safety strap, took the gun in his hand and said, "If you try to leave this elevator, I will shoot you." He said it almost matter-of-factly and routinely, as if he were saying, "Next stop, ladies' apparel and kitchenware."

I was now a federal felon, no longer a free man. I was also scared to death. This was no game. Within minutes, the elevator was filled with four other rabbis and more than a dozen screaming student demonstrators. We were taken down to the basement and whisked into waiting police vans.

RECENTLY, AT A BAR MITZVAH RECEPTION, a man introduced himself to me. He said we had been arrested together. He had been one of the students and had since become a rabbi himself. We reminisced for a while and then he gave me a new ending to the story I had thought was completed over two decades ago.

"There's something I've never told you," he said. "When they brought me, literally kicking and screaming into that freight elevator, I was scared out of my wits. I was about to lose it. But then I saw *your* face and somehow I just knew that everything was going to be O.K."

My face, I thought. You should only know.

Bats

I NEVER SAW A BAT. I hope I never do. One nearly killed a close friend of mine. While he was on a ladder, cleaning a third floor gutter, a bat surprised him. He reflexively jumped backward and landed in a hospital bed for six months.

"That damn bat changed my life," he said. "Gave me all kinds of time to read and just think about what was important. That's when I decided to get involved in the synagogue."

That's how he wound up being chairman of the Rabbi Search Committee. The whole thing makes you wonder. You have some things planned out, but no matter how single-minded you are, other things get mixed in. Things just seem to fly into what you're doing and all you can do is hang on for dear life. Take how I wound up being the rabbi of a congregation in suburban Boston for the past quarter century.

I was about to complete a two-year rabbinic fellowship near Chicago. Karen and I knew only that we hoped to find a small congregation somewhere in the Northeast. I managed to get three interviews: One in Montreal, one on Long Island, one west of Boston. I bought a new suit, went to the barber and got on an airplane. I thought Montreal and Long Island were okay, but they didn't think I was. The third congregation, only a few years old, had already been ravaged by several power struggles over phony religious issues. Colleagues in the area warned me to stay away: "It's a mess."

During the interview, the members of the search committee spent most of their time yelling at one another. When they finished, they started on the young man in the new suit. Believing that the best defense was a good offense, I remember suggesting that a decent rabbi would make it hard for them to go on pretending that they were just another Protestant denomination in a Yankee town. That got their attention. There was more yelling and shouting. The interview ended abruptly with an embarrassed silence.

When I phoned Karen afterward, I didn't even bother going into details: "Forget it, honey. No way is this one gonna happen. Too bad, the chairman is really a beautiful man. It'd be great to work with him, but it wasn't meant to be."

HE WAS AN AMAZING MAN. For a living, he joked to me years later, he sold the government high-tech hardware they didn't really need, so it was relatively easy to sell the congregation a rabbi they didn't really want. When he met me at the airport, during the long ride to the interview, he had made up his mind that I was the rabbi he was looking for. So he drove me on a detour around a much more beautiful, neighboring town and told me that was where the congregation was. He convinced me it would be the opportunity of a lifetime: "People here can go in any direction." He must have done some job on the committee too, because they called me back for a second chance.

This time the discussion was more civil, even polite. It was as if they had never met me before. The chairman led the discussion with great tact and diplomacy. It wasn't until over a decade later that I realize just how much diplomacy. After a few years of my rabbinic leadership, all but three of the original members on the search committee had resigned from the congregation. But miraculously, I still had a job.

Over the years, my friend and I bicycled together and talked politics. I performed the *b'nai mitzvah* of his children. It's been over a decade since he died of cancer. To conduct the funeral of a dear friend, someone so influential in your life, is a sacred honor. I was scheduled to go to Israel when he entered the final stages of the terrible disease. His family and I agreed that if he should die while I was gone, I would return for the funeral. I visited his silent bedside the day before I left. He was on painkillers and barely conscious. Still, I fantasized he might understand what I was saying, but there was no way to be certain. "Thank you for touching my life. If I have failed you or hurt you, please forgive me. I love you."

A week later, upon returning from Israel, I learned that there had been no change. The hospital room was serene in the dim light. I approached the bed almost reverently, but before I could say anything, the unconscious man in the bed before us, suddenly sat straight up. We all jumped back. He stared at us as if he were trying to see, then slowly eased himself down. He said nothing.

"I've never seen anything like it," whispered his nurse. "After such a long span of inaction, to have such energy. Do you suppose he was trying to say goodbye?"

It's funny how people pop into our lives. Often, we don't realize the role they played until long after they've gone. Perhaps it's just as well. If we knew who they'd turn out to be, we might run away or step backward off a ladder.

MOST OF US BELIEVE IN FREE WILL. Most of us however also have known moments when we felt as if we were permitted to survey our lives from such a high vantage point that our freedom was revealed to be illusory. The closer we are to what is happening, the more we believe we are in complete control. The farther away we get, the more we are willing to acknowledge the participation of something greater. We realize that we were part of something much larger than our daily decisions.

Everything is organically, seamlessly joined to everything else. We have been players in a divine scheme, neither marionettes nor zombies but waves in an ocean, dancers in a ballet, colors on a canvas, words in a story. Discrete and probably autonomous, but never entirely independent. Of course, it is preposterous. Of course, it makes no rational sense. But for just a moment, it is as if we encounter our destiny. Everything is *within* God.

This does not mean that we give in and simply "go with the flow." Indeed, what is "set before us" to accomplish frequently requires stubborn, solitary, courageous and "seemingly" voluntary action. But now what we do feels less fragmented than before. Now we understand the strange Talmudic maxim: "All is in the hands of heaven, except the fear of heaven." The only thing truly within our power, and our power alone, may be whether or not we will behave in each moment with arrogance or reverence. Other than that, life goes on as before. The only difference is that now we do what we do with reverence. "In life, unlike in literature," as Professor Uriel Simon of Bar Ilan University has taught, "we cannot always discern the hand of God."

HEAVEN HAS ASSIGNED A ROLE TO EACH OF US. It's the only one we're going to get. Sometimes we don't like our part. We want someone else's lines, costume, entrance. I, for instance, think I should have been assigned the role of starting quarterback for the San Francisco '49ers.

"Sorry, that part's taken. You get to be the rabbi in a small town in Massachusetts. That's the only part we've got for you. You want it or not?"

If we say, "O.K., I'll take the part, I choose to play it with all my strength," then, even though we probably won't make it into the National Football League, it won't matter. We wouldn't take the job even if they coaxed us because we'll be having too much fun being who we are. But if, on the other hand, we sulk or stubbornly try to seize some other actor's part by pretending we're someone else, then we just wind up being a second-rate actor in a "B" movie of our life story.

I COUNSEL MY STUDENTS on the eve of their graduation from rabbinic school, all terrified that they won't get the job they want: "Relax, because God is going to put you where God wants you—whether you like it or not."

Everyone and everything moves within the divine. Even bats.

Conception

BEFORE CLASS, A GROUP OF MY HIGH SCHOOL SENIORS were talking about college entrance essays. Each university comes up with its own creative, literary challenge. The kids agreed the topic that was most fun to write about was choosing someone from the past with whom you'd most like to spend an evening—and explain why. The kids were wonderfully creative. Some had chosen artists, others politicians, one chose Socrates. All of a sudden they turned to me: "Who would you pick?"

Without a moment's hesitation (and to my embarrassed surprise), I said I would pick my father. Even though we had set his body in the earth years ago, he, of all people, would be the most likely to possess information vital to my self-understanding. The person I wanted to spend an evening with was not the old man who had survived a few heart attacks, but the dashing young Naval officer, who had just returned from the South Pacific at the end of World War II, even younger than I am now.

My wife, who is a psychotherapist, says that one of our most difficult tasks is learning how to imagine our parents as real human beings, as ordinary folks. Towards this end, she advises trying to envision who they were when they were our age. What sort of people they would be if they were among our current circle of friends? What would their politics be? What kind of music would they like? What about them would be interesting? And, of course, how would they comprehend the actions of their children?

Freud said it's impossible for a person to imagine his or her own conception. There are things you can believe and understand, but just cannot fathom. Too much of a blow to the ego.

You may be disappointed to realize that your conception may have depended on an extra glass of wine or a few too many beers. You did not, in other words, burst forth a fully formed adult from the head of Zeus. Your mother and father probably didn't even say: "Let us now cohabit and make the perfect human being." They may have wanted a child, but they probably had a good time trying and fell asleep with smiles on their faces when they were done.

MY BROTHER, WHO HAS HIS OWN MISCHIEVOUS REASONS for perpetuating such humbling family legends, swears that our mother once told him that I was conceived after she and my father watched the movie *I'm a Yankee Doodle Dandy*, on a holiday weekend in, of all places, Cleveland. (I really do enjoy the Fourth of July.)

At least I am in good company. According to rabbinic legend, King David, the paradigm Hebrew monarch, author of the book of Psalms and scion of the messianic line, had an unpretentious beginning. David's father, Jesse, separated from his wife for three years after the birth of their sixth son. During that time, he was far from celibate, and tried to seduce one of his female slaves. His wife disguised herself as the girl of Jesse's desire and the old king, completely taken in by the ruse, made love to his own wife without knowing it. The child borne of that union was given out as the son of the slave girl, so Jesse would not discover the trick.

There is a similar story about how Judah impregnated Tamar while she, too, had disguised herself as someone else. The child of that union was Perez, one of Jesse's earlier great-great-grandparents.

In other words, people may think they're having a terrific evening, but God is behind the whole thing. Only after you grow up do you understand that your parents were God's instruments, just like you.

Suicide

IT WAS A WARM THURSDAY MORNING in August. Karen and I had just finished attending a religious education conference on Long Island where I had taught a few classes. When it was over, instead of driving directly back to Boston we took a detour to Brooklyn.

We were trying to find out something about a man named Ferencz Lefkowitz, Karen's paternal grandfather who died in the Bronx in 1917. We don't know much about him. Since Karen's father spent most of his youth in an orphanage, details were scarce. Folks either didn't know about him—or if they did, they wouldn't tell. Much of the information Karen could find was confusing. After emigrating to the United States, why did he return to Europe twice? Why, if some documents say he was an automobile worker, did Aunt Goldie insist he was a musician? And then, Karen got the *pièce de résistance*: A photocopy of his death certificate. Cause of death: "Gunshot wound to the abdomen. Suicide." But if it was a suicide, we wonder, why shoot yourself in the abdomen? (I tease Karen about her crazy Hungarian ancestors.) Maybe there was foul play?

So here we were in the Washington Cemetery in Flatbush, surrounded by the inner city. The graveyard was overgrown, jammed with generations of tombstones of every size and shape. And every name was Jewish. The park had grown across two major highways. And even if we could have managed to shut out the occasional noise of automobile traffic, the old Brighton Beach elevated line roared overhead every fifteen minutes.

The woman in the office told us how to find the grave that no one visited. There wasn't a cloud in the sky nor, as far as we could tell, anyone but the two of us there. After passing row upon row of ornate tombstones, all cluttered with genealogical tidbits, we came to the last row and the end of our hopes. Oh God. Of course. We should have known: He was a suicide. Traditional Judaism taught that someone who threw the gift of life back in the face of the Creator does not deserve a beautiful plot. So suicides are laid to rest at the back edge of the cemetery as a kind of communal reprimand.

But we were not prepared for the impact of this last row. Who knew there were so many? There must have been several hundred small white stones, each no more than a foot high. No more than a few feet apart, so close together, it was inconceivable that they could mark graves of normal width. The stones were tilting, broken. Some had fallen down. Many of the names were barely legible. I remembered the suicides I had buried as a rabbi and the families they left behind, and I was grateful that we are more compassionate today. Karen and I were devastated by—and furious with—the old custom.

Soon we found ourselves standing before what was unmistakably the final resting place of Ferencz Lefkowitz. Ferencz Lefkowitz, who were you? What ever happened to you? Why did you do this?

KAREN AND I HELD ONE ANOTHER. We whispered the *kaddish* memorial prayer and we wept in the August sunshine. I found a pebble for Karen which she placed on the stone of her grandfather.

Ferencz Lefkowitz, without you, my wife would not have been born. Without you, our children would not have been born.

Ferencz Lefkowitz, you who held a gun to your abdomen, your life was not in vain. Believe me.

My reverie was cut short by the roar of the subway overhead. Then, in the bright and cloudless sky, there was silence again.

Making Love

It was the Sabbath morning when we read of how Abraham sent his servant, Eliezer, to find a wife for his son, Isaac. Maybe fifty people had gathered around the big table in the prayer hall in my synagogue. They had come an hour and a half before services and the week's *bar mitzvah* for bagels, coffee and one another's insights into the deeper meanings of the biblical text.

From my seat at the head of the table at these weekly sessions, I called on people who wanted to speak. Seated across from me was a young, Harvard-trained physician, fluent in Chinese, with a degree in acupuncture from Beijing. A new member of the congregation, he had been coming to services every month or so. I congratulated myself that his intuitive spirituality was drawn by my attempts at synthesizing East and West. (He has since become my own physician.)

Also at the table was one of my favorite former rabbinic students. Since the two of us had become friends at school, it was not surprising that when she took an administrative job in the Boston area which left her free on Saturday mornings, she would attend my congregation.

The group was scheduled to continue for another half hour, but I had to excuse myself to meet with the *bar mitzvah* family before services began. I invited someone to continue leading the group and quietly set out to leave the room. Since this is exactly what I do whenever there is a *bar mitzvah* (and since there are *bar mitzvahs* on most mornings), no one paid much attention to my departure. But as I was about to open the door to leave, something came over me. I walked back into the middle of the discussion. It was not easy to do this inconspicuously in a crowd of fifty people. All heads followed my path. I leaned down and whispered into the startled doctor's ear, "Don't look now, but the young woman seated across from you in the gray dress is a rabbi. She is unmarried."

I didn't wait for a response. I just turned around and went to meet with the *bar mitzvah* family.

At the end of the week, I got a bouquet of flowers from the couple. A few months later, I did the wedding.

THIS REMINDS ME OF THE FIRST TIME I visited Karen's home. She gave me a tour of the house and then we took a long walk up and down a beautiful, tree-lined street named Roselawn. Her grandmother lived alone in the apartment upstairs. All the while Karen and I walked, the old woman sat on the upstairs porch and watched us. What was she looking for, I wondered? Later, she confided to her granddaughter that she knew we would be getting married very soon. We were surprised to hear this because at the time, we had only been dating for a few days.

What is it about romantic meetings that evoke the participation of heaven? And old people, how do they know?

RABBI MENAHEM MENDL OF KOTZK, a Hasidic master, suggests a beautiful twist to the Genesis account of how Abraham dispatches his servant, Eliezer, to find a wife for his son Isaac. At the beginning of the story, muses the

"Kotzker," Eliezer secretly hoped he wouldn't find anyone and then Isaac would be free to marry his own daughter. But once Eliezer saw what was coming down, that this whole thing must be coming directly from God, then he understood that Rebecca was *supposed* to marry Isaac. He now realized that he was actually serving One higher than his master. With his ego and secret agenda out of the way, Eliezer was free to accomplish his true mission.

What a mysterious, wonderful and fulfilling experience, to be instrumental in bringing two lovers together. Maybe there *are* marriages made in heaven.

Crossing the Vistula

I AM USUALLY THE FIRST FACULTY MEMBER to arrive at the college where I teach on Thursday mornings, so I was delighted and surprised to also find there the man who, for many years, has been my teacher. It was a brutally cold day and the windchill had turned the canyons of Manhattan into tundra. There we were, I in my high-tech down parka and he in an ankle-length fur coat and Russian hat. Since he had always been drawn to eccentric outfits, I was not surprised. The last time I had invited him to speak to my congregation, he showed up in a green, plaid sports jacket. When I gave him a quizzical glance, he explained that when he saw it on the rack it had whispered, "Buy me. Buy me, please." So he did.

His outfit reminded me of one of the most beautiful Sabbath days of my life. About a quarter of a century ago, when I was one of his students, he had asked me to join him and some members of his congregation who studied together on Sabbath afternoons at an estate overlooking Long Island Sound.

Our learning ended an hour or so before sunset and the departure of the Sabbath. He invited me to take a walk with him in the snow and the cold yellow light before the *havdalah* ceremony marking the end of the day. He was wearing a big fur coat that day, too, and he looked like a Polish Rebbe. We trudged through the driven snow and the vanishing sunlight. All I remember is his teaching presence and a kind of joke he made: "Here we are, Larry, crossing the frozen River Vistula."

Seeing him in front of the college in his fur coat brought it all back to me and I told him about the River Vistula. But he only smiled and, without missing a beat, said, "And the only reason I said it then was so that we could share this sweet memory now."

It occurs to me that we have here a new subcategory of déjà vu. It is not that we have the strange sensation of having been here before, but rather the even stranger sensation of, for at least a moment, understanding why we were where we were.

NOWADAYS, THE SACRED USUALLY MASQUERADES as "coincidence." We become aware of some greater network of which we suddenly seem to have always been a part all along. We glimpse at why we were created. The coincidences can take myriad forms. We can simply be shocked to discover that what we have been doing fits into some larger constellation of meaning. We can suddenly sense the presence of a network of mutual interdependence binding us to others. Or, we can understand for a moment why something happened many years ago. Among my generation, there is even a melody which we jokingly hum as a way of saying, "Something very big is happening and we have just had a glimpse." It is the theme song from the old television program, *The Twilight Zone.*

Zaddok HaKohen of Lublin, a Hasidic master, taught that "the first premise of faith is to believe that there is no such thing as happenstance. . . .Every detail, small or great, they are all from the Holy One."

The Silver Screen

WE ALL MOVE BACKWARD AND FORWARD in our years. Not so much seeing the future or remembering the past, but understanding suddenly how they are joined together through the stories we are busy writing with the words we say and the things we do. Sometimes the past intrudes as a nuisance; other times we realize that we can reenter our past and strike up a conversation with who we used to be.

In a scene near the end of Alfred Hitchcock's *North by Northwest*, set in the tourist cafeteria beneath Mount Rushmore, Eva Marie Saint is supposed to fake shooting Cary Grant to convince the evil James Mason of her loyalty. If you watch the luncheon crowd in the background closely, just as Eva Marie pulls the gun from her purse, you will notice a little boy. He couldn't be more than nine years old. He is having lunch with his back to the action. Unfortunately, however, he has rehearsed the scene one too many times. We know this because he covers his ears about ten seconds before the gun is fired. He's been through it all before. At least in this scene, for him there are no surprises. He's just waiting for it to happen so he can get on with his lunch. When he gets a little older, he will learn that these "replays" are not interruptions, but gifts.

IN HIS NOVEL, *THE RIGHT STUFF*, Tom Wolfe chronicles the beginnings of America's manned space flight program. One of the early scenes in the movie version takes place in the

Mojave desert at a tavern where those early test pilots hung out after the day's work. The bartender was a crusty old coot who served up drinks and sage quips to the men who had the right stuff. One of those pilots was the young Chuck Yeager, played by Sam Shepard, a handsome swashbuckling, horse-riding pilot, chasing the gremlins who lived beyond the sound barrier. The man playing the bartender and counseling the young Chuck Yeager is the real life Chuck Yeager.

Is there anything you would like to tell the person who is now playing the person who you were several decades ago?

Act of God

ABOUT SEVENTEEN YEARS AGO, as was our family's custom back in the days when the children were young, we would all go out for dinner at Burger King. (For us, in those years, it qualified as "dinner at a restaurant.") On the way home, if we had a little time and a little money, we might stop at Marshall's, a discount clothing store. The kids would play hide-and-seek among the racks of clothing and Karen and I would browse for bargains.

On one such evening, I caught a glimpse of a tall, carefully made-up, attractive woman out of the corner of my eye. She seemed, even at first glance, to be distraught. Pretending not to notice her as she moved into the aisle where I stood, I saw that she was very pregnant and accompanied by a man. They were discreetly moving toward me and she was trying to catch my eye. But even if she did, I would have feigned ignorance. Yes, I know, I'm a rabbi, a public person, but, gimme a break, this public person happens to be shopping for clothes.

It didn't work. She was closing in and moving through the bright fluorescent lights and Muzak like a guided missile.

"Aren't you Rabbi Kushner?"

I could lie. But instead I answered, "Yes, I am. Have we met?"

"Not exactly, we attended a service you did. My husband and I thought you were very nice."

But before I could even acknowledge her compliment, she moved in for the kill.

"Oh Rabbi, we were at the doctor's this afternoon. The third opinion. He says I have an inoperable tumor. I'm going to die. He says that the baby will be fine," she added, holding her belly, "but I've only got six months at the most."

Her husband was trying to look strong, but his eyes seemed abnormally red.

"Oh, my God! I'm sorry. Is there anything I can do?"

(Stupid question. "Sure, a miracle maybe—right here between sweaters and men's slacks. Nothing big, mind you, just let her live to see her kid grow up." Something like that.)

"Hey dad, could I buy this T-shirt with a picture of Superman on it?"

"Not now, son. Go find mom. I have to talk to these people. It's important."

They introduced themselves, gave me the details. They'd been thinking about joining my congregation. Their world had collapsed. Why has this happened? Would I do the funeral?

They joined.

She bore a daughter.

She died.

I did the funeral.

THERE ARE TWO WAYS TO UNDERSTAND our relationship with God: God can be above us or we can be within God. In the first, it is possible for us to have a relationship *with* God. There are two discrete parties who can each behave freely and independently. And since God is *other* than the world, there must be some things which are *not* God: A devil, an evil instinct, the "dark side of the force." Evil has its own independent existence. It is in business for itself.

In the second model, we are *within* God; we are one with God. God is everywhere and everything. All being derives its reality from God. According to this paradigm, if God is within all creation, then what *appears* as evil can only be a distant, albeit distorted, expression of the divine. This doesn't make it "good." But nothing can be entirely separate from or independent of God. Everything, therefore, is the way it is "supposed" to be.

At the end of the Book of Job, God shows Job the whole awesome pageant of life and death: Lions tearing apart gazelles. Vultures ripping flesh. Thunderstorms. Earthquakes. Everything. Then God says to Job, in effect, "What do you think of that, huh? I hope you like it, 'cause I'm in that too." Not just in feeling good. But *everything*.

The stories with happy endings distract our attention from all the other painful stories. They say to us that somehow things work out, even though it often seems like they don't. For a moment, it seems possible that our grief may be due only to our own myopia.

The seeds of the giant redwoods, after all, are capable of germinating only once they have been through the intense heat of a forest fire.

NOT LONG AGO, I WAS SITTING WITH THE OTHER MEMBERS of my synagogue's high school faculty over a Monday night pizza supper. We were surveying the students. Even after a long day of school, their energy astonished us. My glance settled on a short, vivacious, red-haired girl of seventeen. I pretended I was not looking; I did not mean to intrude on their fun. She had just finished telling a joke or playing some kind of prank. Her face had a grin as irrepressible as the sunrise. Everyone laughed with her. She is popular. The group erupted with joy. A few minutes later, she came over to our table and asked if I would read over a creative worship service she had written for an upcoming youth conclave.

"Why not? I need a good laugh," I said with a wink.

I love that girl. I am honored that she looks up to me. That girl's father never did remarry.

"Last week," I whispered to another teacher, "her dad told me that his daughter was thinking of becoming a rabbi."

Look, I don't think God made a tumor grow in that girl's mother's brain or that God has anything to do with the choice of careers or where I used to shop for bargain basement clothes. But I can't get it out of my head that somehow God is mixed up in the whole horrible, holy and joyous goddamn thing.

Tunnel Vision

I was driving home from Logan Airport through the Sumner Tunnel under Boston Harbor. I should say, I was *trying* to drive home. Even under ordinary conditions, making it into the tunnel can be harrowing. Seven lanes of traffic become two. In rush hour it is bad. In the dark, it is even worse. And in snow, you can kiss dinnertime goodbye. So there I was, watching the blurred patterns of red brake lights through the peep hole that was once a transparent windshield, creeping forward, inching forward. Too fast, you hit someone. Too slow, everyone cuts in front of you. It can do funny things to a person's mind.

I should have realized something odd was coming down when I absentmindedly read a bumper sticker on the car in front of me which looked like it read: "Free Ferencz Lefkowitz." (Ferencz Lefkowitz was my wife's paternal grandfather. He died of a gunshot wound to the abdomen. I once visited his grave in Brooklyn. Maybe he shared the name with some kind of freedom fighter.)

When, at last, my turn came for the privilege of being able to drive past the toll collector in the green booth, I was again startled. This time by the man's face. Normally, a driver might not even make eye contact. A hand passes a dollar bill to another hand. But with such congestion, drivers and toll collectors have time to actually look at one another for a few seconds. We were both momentarily embarrassed by each other's gaze. I made some kind of Boston driver's long-

140

suffering face that said, "Hey, it's the Sumner Tunnel in rush hour, what can you do?" He left the monotony of his job long enough to commiserate and long enough for me to become convinced that I had seen him somewhere before. Then it hit me. This guy looks exactly like Charlie Slocum, a retired biology teacher I met up in Glacier National park decades ago. Could he possibly be the same man? No, he loved the outdoors too much to get caught working rush hour traffic in a glass booth.

My reverie was cut short: Now the squeeze began, each driver jockeying for a slot in one of the two tunnel lanes. Here, you must be especially careful of what is on either side of you. I am dimly aware that the bus next to me seems awfully old, more like an antique. I can't seem to make out the advertisements on its side. Well, of course I can't. They're written in German. SS officers are walking down the aisle. They seem to be examining the papers of the disgruntled passengers. I'm almost at the tunnel now.

What's going on here? Are these people really out there, in the snow, in the evening rush hour, caught with me at the entrance to the tunnel? Or are they the random fantasies of a man caught in commuter hell pushing the envelope of his own sanity?

Of course, I know the difference between imagination and reality. Reality is what you can't control. Imagination is where you are a god unto yourself. But if I'm one with God, if the borders of myself are dissolved in the evening snow so that it is momentarily impossible to determine where I end and where the pavement begins and God is the One uniting all Creation, then things could get pretty interesting. We are down to five lanes.

Relax: This never happened to me. I never saw a bumper sticker with the name of my wife's paternal grandfather on it. Nor did I ever see anyone who looked like Charlie Slocum in the Sumner Tunnel. I don't even remember what Charlie looked like. That's not even his real name. I'm making this whole thing up. I'm just trying to push interconnectedness to its ultimate expression. These characters—Charlie Slocum, my student, Shifra's great aunt Sussie, Ferencz Lefkowitz, Miriam Kushner, Rabbi Menahem Mendl Morgenstern of Kotzk—they're all here, all the time. So are all the others I've forgotten or repressed or never knew. Everyone who ever lived. Everything that ever was. They're all present and connected, pulling, tugging, tickling, feeding, shouting, shooting, loving one another. The primary job of a story is to arrange a few of them into a verbal bouquet so that we may, from a safe distance, contemplate them in their relationship, their interdependence.

"Please pass the potatoes," one says to another, backstage.

"Am I 'on' yet?"

"No, wait until this story's over. Who are you?"

We can't fit everyone into one coherent, linear plot. We have not yet figured out a way to tell more than one story at a time—as it happens in life.

Professor Uriel Simon said, "In life, unlike in literature, we cannot always discern the hand of God."

And I say, "In life, unlike in literature, we can live several stories at once. Maybe we can live them all."

But we can, of course, as has become popular during the past decade in a spate of prime time soaps, interweave a half dozen subplots into one larger sixty-minute episode.

But even then it's basically one at a time. If you're a clever screenwriter, you can give a few characters walk-on parts in other subplots so as to help integrate everything. The man behind me honks. (Is *he* in this story too? Perhaps his wife in labor. Maybe he's just picked up a young man who's interviewing to become the rabbi of his congregation. Maybe he's a serial murderer. Who knows?)

My colleague, Rabbi Ed Feld, once observed that the reason everyone is so confused about what really happened on Mount Sinai is because the Five Books of Moses actually contain at least a half dozen conflicting accounts. In one version, you can't get too close to God lest you die. In another version, seventy elders have lunch with God. In yet another version, God thunders from the heavens; while in a different account, the divine voice whispers from deep inside each person.

It's not that the editor of the text did a sloppy job of weaving mutually exclusive accounts, says Feld. It's that the editor understood the multifaceted nature of reality and wisely, brilliantly chose to convey this in such a way as to leave the reader in the same state of confusion about what "really" happened (as if reality were only one thing at a time) that those who lived through it were in.

The correct answer is: "All of the above." Everything happened and it all happened at once. And everyone was there. But since that's too hard to explain, I'll tell you a story: Once I was driving home from Logan Airport through the Sumner Tunnel...

The Last Word

My mother, who turned eighty more than a few years ago, tells me that as you get older, it only gets worse: "No matter what you say, God always has the last word." That strikes me as wise, especially from a woman who has refined to high art the skill of getting in the last word. But it does make me wonder: What exactly is the "last word"?

If you and God have been adversaries, then the last word might be a triumphalist, "I'm God. You're not." Or, even worse, "I'm God. You're dead." If you've been friends and developed a good working relationship, the last word might be, "Thanks for all your help." But if, after all those years, you've come to understand God as "The Infinite One of whom you are a finite dimension, a unique but fleeting expression, then it would be, "I'm God. So are you." Or maybe just, "What took you so long?"

(But, of course, with all distinctions gone, the idea of a "conversation" is itself only a confusing metaphor: What can a wave say to the ocean? What can the ocean say to a wave?)

Before we begin our journey, we are one with all Creation. Once life begins, we find ourselves discrete, individuated, autonomous. And after the journey ends, God gets the last word: "Welcome." With some luck, we get glimmers of the great unity even during our lifetime. We realize that our life—and everything else—has all been part of the divine organism all along, that things are turning out "just the way God intends."

This is not to say that God is running the world like some overextended, occasionally under-performing puppeteer, depriving us of our freedom or moral responsibility. God is simply within all of it. And when we become aware of this, as we do during moments of great meaning or insight, it is as if God were the One who unites (and therefore runs) everything. Questions of free will and determinism become meaningless.

Everything exists within and derives its reality from God, including us. We are dimensions of the divine psyche, seeking to become fully self-aware. And, when we raise our consciousness, we not only realize that we have never really been apart from our divine Source at all, we realize that we also participate in the process itself. You may not be able to have an intimate relationship with such a God, but you are its pride and joy, its best hope.

My colleague, Rabbi Nehemiah Polen, taught me that the world simply is. It is the way it is supposed to be, the way it must be. Such a vision is achieved by a surrender of the ego, by submerging your self in the enveloping waters of divine being. We say the last word, "Oh my God!" to the universe and lose ourselves as we do so.

BEING IS NOT FROM OR BY GOD. IT IS OF GOD. There is only one player: God. In the words of Deuteronomy: "The Lord alone is God: There is nothing else!"

ALL THEOLOGY is autobiography.

Acknowledgments

THERE ARE PEOPLE WHO CARE ENOUGH to try to help an author see the difference between cliché and creativity. They stand invisible behind all these stories. Without such accomplices, there would be no book.

First and foremost is Arthur Magida who patiently edited and re-edited all these pages. He has kept me on track and taught me how to listen for my own voice.

I am grateful to the diligent staff at Jewish Lights Publishing, especially Sandra Korinchak and Theresa Jones Vyhnal, who have brought to this project tireless enthusiasm and originality.

My friends Anita Diamant, Bill Novak and David Mamet have carefully read early versions of these stories and offered invaluable advice and support.

I especially want to thank Stuart Matlins, publisher of Jewish Lights, who believes with all his heart that the task of making books means bringing more light to darkness. He has been both a teacher and a friend.

But, above all, it has been my life-partner, Karen, who, despite all the evidence to the contrary, through her stubborn belief that I have something worthwhile to say, makes writing possible. Like Borowitz taught at our wedding: She is for me a well of living waters.

This book and its jacket were designed by the author.
They were produced in Adobe PageMaker 6.0, Illustrator 4.0, and Photoshop 3.0.
They were transferred to film by MicroPrint, Waltham, Massachusetts.
The jacket was printed by Phoenix Color Corp., Hingham, Massachusetts.
The book was printed and bound by Book Press, Brattleboro, Vermont.

The text face is Minion, designed by Robert Slimbach
and issued in digital form by Adobe systems,
Mountain View, California, in 1989.

For People of All Faiths, All Backgrounds
ABOUT JEWISH LIGHTS PUBLISHING

People of all faiths and backgrounds yearn for books that attract, engage, educate and spiritually inspire.

Our books focus on the issue of the quest for the self, seeking meaning in life. They are books that help all people to better understand who they are and who they might become as a person who is part of a tradition that has its roots in the Judeo-Christian world. They deal with issues of personal growth. They deal with issues of religious inspiration.

We bring to you authors who are at the forefront of spiritual thought and experience. While each has something different to say, they all say it in a voice that you can hear.

Our books are designed to welcome you and then to engage, stimulate and inspire. We judge our success not only by whether or not our books are beautiful and commercially successful, but by whether or not they make a difference in your life.

Given our name and subject matter, the tendency is immediately to pigeonhole us as "another publisher of Jewish books." As we are publishing books of a type that, in many cases, have not been published before, it is hard to find a simple category in which to place us.

We recognize that it is difficult to communicate this difference to a world that is used simply to categorizing things as "Jewish books" or "Judaica." We don't think of ourselves in either of those categories. We describe ourselves as publishing books that reflect the Jewish wisdom tradition for people of all faiths, all backgrounds.

...The Kushner Series

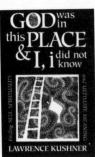

GOD WAS IN THIS PLACE & I, i DID NOT KNOW
Finding Self, Spirituality & Ultimate Meaning
by *Lawrence Kushner*

Who am I? Who is God? Kushner creates inspiring interpretations of Jacob's dream in Genesis, opening a window into Jewish spirituality for people of all faiths and backgrounds.

In a fascinating blend of scholarship, imagination, psychology and history, seven Jewish spiritual masters ask and answer fundamental questions of human experience.

"A brilliant fabric of classic rabbinic interpretations, Hasidic insights and literary criticism which warms us and sustains us."
—*Dr. Norman J. Cohen, Dean, Hebrew Union College, NY*

"Rich and intriguing." —*M. Scott Peck, M.D., author of* The Road Less Traveled

6"x 9", 192 pp. Quality Paperback, ISBN 1-879045-33-8 **$16.95**
6" x 9", 192 pp. Hardcover, ISBN 1-879045-05-2 **$21.95**

HONEY FROM THE ROCK
by *Lawrence Kushner*

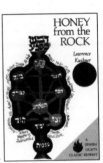

"Quite simply the easiest introduction to Jewish mysticism you can read."

An introduction to the ten gates of Jewish mysticism and how it applies to daily life.

"*Honey from the Rock* captures the flavor and spark of Jewish mysticism. . . . Read it and be rewarded." —*Elie Wiesel*

"A work of love, lyrical beauty, and prophetic insight. "
—*Father Malcolm Boyd*, The Christian Century

6"x 9", 168 pp. Quality Paperback, ISBN 1-879045-02-8 **$14.95**

THE RIVER OF LIGHT
Spirituality, Judaism, Consciousness
by *Lawrence Kushner*

A "manual" for all spiritual travelers who would attempt a spiritual journey in our times. Taking us step by step, Kushner allows us to discover the meaning of our own quest: "to allow the river of light—the deepest currents of consciousness—to rise to the surface and animate our lives."

"Philosophy and mystical fantasy...exhilarating speculative flights launched from the Bible....Anybody—Jewish, Christian, or otherwise...will find this book an intriguing experience."
—*The Kirkus Reviews*
"A very important book."—*Rabbi Adin Steinsaltz*

6"x 9", 180 pp. Quality Paperback, ISBN 1-879045-03-6 **$14.95**

Spirituality

INVISIBLE LINES OF CONNECTION
Sacred Stories of the Ordinary
by *Lawrence Kushner*

Through his everyday encounters with family, friends, colleagues and strang
Kushner takes us deeply into our lives, finding flashes of spiritual insight in
process. Such otherwise ordinary moments as fighting with his children, sh
ping for bargain basement clothes, or just watching a movie are revealed to
touchstones for the sacred.

This is a book where literature meets spirituality, where the sacred meets the o
nary, and, above all, where people of all faiths, all backgrounds can meet
another and themselves. Kushner ties together the stories of our lives into a roadmap showing h
everything "ordinary" is supercharged with meaning—*if* we can just see it.

"Does something both more and different than instruct—it inspirits. Wonderful stories,
from the best storyteller I know."
— David Mamet

"Kushner yet again proves himself both a man of great wisdom and a great writer.
No one can match him in catching glimpses of the Holy."
— M. Scott Peck, M.D., author of *The Road Less Traveled*
and other works

6" x 9", 160 pp. Hardcover, ISBN 1-879045-52-4 **$21.95**

HOW TO BE A PERFECT STRANGER
A Guide to Etiquette in Other People's Religious Ceremonies
Edited by *Arthur J. Magida*

Explains the rituals and celebrations of America's major religions/denomina-
tions, helping an interested guest to feel comfortable, participate to the fullest
extent possible, and avoid violating anyone's religious principles.

"The things Miss Manners forgot to tell us about religion."
— Los Angeles Times

"Concise, informative, and eminently practical."
— Rev. Christopher Leighton, Executive Director,
Institute for Christian-Jewish Studies

6" x 9", 432 pp. Hardcover, ISBN 1-879045-39-7 **$24.95**

SPIRITUALITY...OTHER BOOKS:

Embracing the Covenant: Converts to Judaism Talk about Why
Edited by Rabbi Allan Berkowitz and Patti Moskovitz. 6 x 9, 184 pp (est), Quality Pb,
ISBN 1-879045-50-8 $15.95

Finding Joy: A Practical Spiritual Guide to Happiness
by Dannel Schwartz with Mark Hass. 6 x 9, 192 pp (est), HC, ISBN 1-879045-53-2 $19.95

Godwrestling—Round 2: Ancient Wisdom, Future Paths
by Arthur Waskow. 6 x 9, 352 pp, HC, ISBN 1-879045-45-1 $23.95

God & the Big Bang: Discovering Harmony between Science and Spirituality
by Daniel C. Matt. 6 x 9, 208 pp (est), HC, ISBN 1-879045-48-6 $21.95

Tormented Master: The Life and Spiritual Quest of Rabbi Nahman of Bratslav
by Arthur Green. 6 x 9, 408 pp, Quality Pb, ISBN 1-879045-11-7 $17.95

Your Word Is Fire: The Hasidic Masters on Contemplative Prayer
Edited & transl. by Arthur Green & Barry W. Holtz. 6 x 9, 152 pp, Quality Pb,
ISBN 1-879045-25-7 $14.95

Spirituality

BEING GOD'S PARTNER
How to Find the Hidden Link
Between Spirituality and Your Work

by Jeffrey K. Salkin Introduction by *Norman Lear*

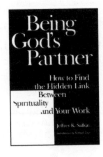

A book that will challenge people of every denomination to reconcile the cares of work and soul. A groundbreaking book about spirituality and the work world, from a Jewish perspective. Helps the reader find God in the ethical striving and search for meaning in the professions and in business. Looks at our modern culture of workaholism and careerism, and offers practical suggestions for balancing your professional life and spiritual self.

Being God's Partner will inspire people of all faiths and no faith to find greater meaning in their work, and see themselves doing God's work in the world.

> "The book is engaging, easy to read and hard to put down—and it will make a difference and change people."
> — Jacob Neusner, Distinguished Research Professor of Religious Studies, University of South Florida

6" x 9", 192 pp. Hardcover, ISBN 1-879045-37-0 **$19.95**

SELF, STRUGGLE & CHANGE
Family Conflict Stories in Genesis
and Their Healing Insights for Our Lives
by *Norman J. Cohen*

How do I find greater wholeness in my life and in my family's life?

The stress of late-20th-century living only brings new variations to timeless personal struggles. The people described by the biblical writers of Genesis were in situations and relationships very much like our own. We identify with them. Their stories still speak to us because they are about the same problems we deal with every day.

A modern master of biblical interpretation brings us greater understanding of the ancient text and of ourselves in this intriguing re-telling of conflict between husband and wife, father and son, brothers, and sisters.

> "Delightfully written ... rare erudition, sensitivity and insight."
> — Elie Wiesel

6" x 9", 224 pp. Hardcover, ISBN 1-879045-19-2 **$21.95**

THE EMPTY CHAIR: FINDING HOPE & JOY
Timeless Wisdom from a Hasidic Master,
Rebbe Nachman of Breslov

Adapted by *Moshe Mykoff* and *the Breslov Research Institute*

A "little treasure" of aphorisms and advice for living joyously and spiritually today, written 200 years ago, but startlingly fresh in meaning and use. Challenges and helps us to move from stress and sadness to hope and joy.

Teacher, guide and spiritual master—Rebbe Nachman provides vital words of inspiration and wisdom for life today for people of any faith, or of no faith.

> "For anyone of any faith, this is a book of healing and wholeness, of being alive!"
> — Bookviews

4" x 6", 128 pp., 2-color text, Hardcover, ISBN 1-879045-16-8 **$9.95**

Theology & Philosophy

FAITH AFTER THE HOLOCAUST?

THE SPIRIT OF RENEWAL
Finding Faith After the Holocaust
by *Edward Feld*

"Boldly redefines the landscape of Jewish religious thought after the Holocaust."
— *Rabbi Lawrence Kushner*

Trying to understand the Holocaust and addressing the question of faith after the Holocaust, Rabbi Feld explores three key cycles of destruction and recovery in Jewish history, each of which radically reshaped Jewish understanding of God, people, and the world.

"Undoubtedly the most moving book I have read....'Must' reading."
— *Rabbi Howard A. Addison*, Conservative Judaism

"A profound meditation on Jewish history [and the Holocaust]....Christians, as well as many others, need to share in this story."
— *The Rt. Rev. Frederick H. Borsch, Ph.D.*, Episcopal Bishop of L.A.

6"x 9", 224 pp. Quality Paperback, ISBN 1-879045-40-0 **$16.95**   HC, ISBN-06-0 **$22.95**

SEEKING THE PATH TO LIFE
Theological Meditations On God and the Nature of People, Love, Life and Death

•AWARD WINNER

by *Rabbi Ira F. Stone*
Ornamentation by *Annie Stone*

For people who never thought they would read a book of theology—let alone understand it, enjoy it, savor it and have it affect the way they think about their lives.

In 45 intense meditations, each a page or two in length, Stone takes us on explorations of the most basic human struggles: life and death, love and anger, peace and war, covenant and exile.

"Wonderful...lyrical...Gives words to the human struggle to find God in the midst of the chaos of modern life."

—*Library Journal*

"A bold book....The reader of any faith will be inspired, challenged and led more deeply into their own encounter with God."

— *The Rev. Carla Berkedal*, Episcopal Priest,
Executive Director of Earth Ministry

6"x 9", 132 pp. Quality Paperback, ISBN 1-879045-47-8 **$14.95**

THEOLOGY & PHILOSOPHY...Other books:

Aspects of Rabbinic Theology
by Solomon Schechter. 6 x 9, 440 pp, Quality Paperback, ISBN 1-879045-24-9 $18.95

The Earth Is the Lord's: The Inner World of the Jew in Eastern Europe
by Abraham Joshua Heschel. 5.5 x 8, 112 pp, Quality Paperback, ISBN 1-879045-42-7 $12.95

The Last Trial: On the Legends and Lore of the Command to Abraham to Offer Isaac as a Sacrific
by Shalom Spiegel. 6 x 9, 208 pp, Quality Paperback, ISBN 1-879045-29-X $17.95

A Passion for Truth: Despair and Hope in Hasidism
by Abraham Joshua Heschel. 5.5 x 8, 352 pp, Quality Paperback, ISBN 1-879045-41-9 $18.95

Self-Help/Recovery

elve Jewish Steps to Recovery: A Personal Guide to Turning from Alcoholism & Other Addictions
Dr. Kerry M. Olitzky & Stuart A. Copans, M.D. 6 x 9, 136 pp,
ality Paperback, ISBN 1-879045-09-5 $12.95   HC, ISBN 1-879045-08-7 $19.95

:overy from Codependence: A Jewish Twelve Steps Guide to Healing Your Soul
Dr. Kerry M. Olitzky. 6 x 9, 160 pp,
ality Paperback, ISBN 1-879045-32-X $13.95   HC, ISBN 1-879045-27-3 $21.95

newed Each Day: Daily Twelve Step Recovery Meditations Based on the Bible
Dr. Kerry M. Olitzky & Aaron Z. Vol. I, Genesis & Exodus, 224 pp; Vol. II, Leviticus, Numbers &
iteronomy, 280 pp; Two-Volume Set, Quality Paperback, ISBN 1-879045-21-4 $27.90

ie Hundred Blessings Every Day: Daily Twelve Step Recovery Affirmations, Exercises for Personal
owth & Renewal Reflecting Seasons of the Jewish Year
Dr. Kerry M. Olitzky. 4.5 x 6.5, 432 pp, Quality Paperback, ISBN 1-879045-30-3 $14.95

aling of Soul, Healing of Body: Spiritual Leaders Unfold the Strength & Solace in Psalms
ited by Rabbi Simkha Y. Weintraub, CSW for the Jewish Healing Center. 6 x 9, 2-color text, 128 pp,
ality Paperback, ISBN 1-879045-31-1 $14.95

Lifecycle

r/Bat Mitzvah Basics: A Practical Family Guide to Coming of Age Together
ited by Cantor Helen Leneman. 6 x 9, 184 pp (est),
C, ISBN 1-879045-51-6 $24.95   Quality Pb, ISBN 1-879045-54-0 $16.95

anukkah by Dr. Ron Wolfson. 7 x 9, 192 pp, Quality Paperback, ISBN 1-870945-97-4 $14.95

fecycles, Vol. 1: Jewish Women on Life Passages & Personal Milestones
ited by Rabbi Debra Orenstein. 6 x 9, 480 pp, HC, ISBN 1-879045-14-1 $24.95

fecycles, Vol. 2: Jewish Women on Biblical & Contemporary Life Themes
. by Rabbi Debra Orenstein & Rabbi Jane Litman. 6 x 9, 480 pp,
C, ISBN 1-879045-15-X $24.95 Available July 1995

ourning & Mitzvah: A Guided Journal to Walking the Mourner's Path Through Grief to Healing
 Anne Brener. 7.5 x 9, 288 pp, Quality Paperback, ISBN 1-879045-23-0 $19.95

ie New Jewish Baby Book: Names, Ceremonies, Customs—A Guide for Today's Families
 Anita Diamant. 6 x 9, 328 pp, Quality Paperback, ISBN 1-879045-28-1 $15.95

he Passover Seder by Dr. Ron Wolfson. 7 x 9, 336 pp,
uality Paperback, ISBN 1-879045-93-1 $14.95

utting God on the Guest List: How to Reclaim the Spiritual Meaning of Your Child's Bar or Bat
itzvah by Jeffrey K. Salkin. 6 x 9, 184 pp,
uality Paperback ISBN 1-879045-10-9 $14.95 HC ISBN 1-879045-20-6 $21.95

he Shabbat Seder by Dr. Ron Wolfson. 7 x 9, 272 pp,
uality Paperback, ISBN 1-879045-90-7 $14.95

o That Your Values Live On: Ethical Wills & How to Prepare Them
dited by Jack Riemer & Nathaniel Stampfer. 6 x 9, 272 pp,
uality Paperback, ISBN 1-879045-34-6 $16.95   HC, ISBN 1-879045-07-9 $23.95

 Time to Mourn, A Time to Comfort: A Guide to Jewish Bereavement and Comfort
 Dr. Ron Wolfson. 7 x 9, 320 pp, Quality Paperback, ISBN 1-879045-96-6 $16.95

Vhen a Grandparent Dies: A Kid's Own Remembering Workbook for
ealing with Shiva and the Year Beyond by Nechama Liss-Levinson, Ph.D. 8 x 10, 2-color text, 48 pp,
IC, ISBN 1-879045-44-3 $14.95

Children's

BUT GOD REMEMBERED
Stories of Women from Creation to the Promised Land
by *Sandy Eisenberg Sasso*

Full color illustrations by *Bethanne Andersen*

NON-SECTARIAN, NON-DENOMINATIONAL.
A fascinating collection of four different stories of women only briefly mentioned in biblical tradition and religious texts, but never before explored. Award-winning author Sasso brings to life the intriguing stories of Lilith, Serach, Bityah, and the Daughters of Z, courageous and strong women from ancient tradition. All teach important values through their faith and actions.

For ages 8 and up

"Exquisite....a book of beauty, strength and spirituality."
—Association of Bible Teachers

9" x 12", 32 pp. Hardcover, Full color illus., ISBN 1-879045-43-5 **$16.95**

IN GOD'S NAME
For ages 4-8

by *Sandy Eisenberg Sasso*
Full color illustrations by *Phoebe Stone*

MULTICULTURAL, NON-SECTARIAN, NON-DENOMINATIONAL.
Like an ancient myth in its poetic text and vibrant illustrations, this mod[e] fable about the search for God's name celebrates the diversity and, at the sa[me] time, the unity of all the people of the world. Each seeker claims he or she al[one] knows the answer. Finally, they come together and learn what God's na[me] really is, sharing the ultimate harmony of belief in one God by people of [all] faiths, all backgrounds.

• AWARD WINNER •

"I got goose bumps when I read *In God's Name*, its language and illustrations are that moving. This is a book children will love and the whole family will cherish for its beauty and power."
—Francine Klagsbrun, author of *Mixed Feelings: Love, Hate, Rivalry, and Reconciliation among Brothers and Sisters*

"What a lovely, healing book!"
—Madeleine L'Engle

| Selected by Parent Council Ltd.™ |

9" x 12", 32 pp. Hardcover, Full color illus., ISBN 1-879045-26-5 **$16.95**

For children K-4
GOD'S PAINTBRUSH
by *Sandy Eisenberg Sasso*
Full color illustrations by *Annette Compton*

MULTICULTURAL, NON-SECTARIAN, NON-DENOMINATIONAL.
Invites children of all faiths and backgrounds to encounter God openly in their own lives. Wonderfully interactive, provides questions adult and child can explore together at the end of each episode.

"An excellent way to honor the imaginative breadth and depth of the spiritual life of the young."
—Dr. Robert Coles, Harvard University

• AWARD WINNER •

11" x 8½", 32 pp. Hardcover, Full color illustrations, ISBN 1-879045-22-2 **$16.95**

THE 11TH COMMANDMENT
Wisdom from Our Children
by The Children of America

MULTICULTURAL, NON-SECTARIAN, NON-DENOMINATIONAL.

"If there were an Eleventh Commandment, what would it be?"
Children of many religious denominations across America answer this question—in their own drawings and words—in *The 11th Commandment*. This full-color collection of "Eleventh Commandments" reveals kids' ideas about how people should respond to God.

8" x 10", 48 pp. Hardcover, Full color illustrations, ISBN 1-879045-46-X **$16.95**

_____	Aspects of Rabbinic Theology (pb), $18.95	_____
_____	Bar/Bat Mitzvah Basics (hc), $24.95; (pb), $16.95	_____
_____	Being God's Partner (hc), $19.95	_____
_____	But God Remembered (hc), $16.95	_____
_____	The Earth Is the Lord's (pb), $12.95	_____
_____	The 11th Commandment (hc), $16.95	_____
_____	Embracing the Covenant (pb), $15.95	_____
_____	The Empty Chair (hc), $9.95	_____
_____	Finding Joy (hc), $19.95	_____
_____	God & the Big Bang (hc), $21.95	_____
_____	God's Paintbrush (hc), $16.95	_____
_____	Godwrestling—Round 2 (hc), $23.95	_____
_____	Hanukkah (pb), $14.95	_____
_____	Healing of Soul, Healing of Body (pb), $14.95	_____
_____	How to Be a Perfect Stranger (hc), $24.95	_____
_____	In God's Name (hc), $16.95	_____
_____	The Last Trial (pb), $17.95	_____
_____	Lifecycles, Volume 1 (hc), $24.95	_____
_____	Lifecycles, Volume 2 (hc), $24.95	_____
_____	Mourning & Mitzvah (pb), $19.95	_____
_____	The NEW Jewish Baby Book (pb), $15.95	_____
_____	One Hundred Blessings Every Day, (pb), $14.95	_____
_____	A Passion for Truth (pb), $18.95	_____
_____	Passover Seder (pb), $14.95	_____
_____	Putting God on the Guest List (hc), $21.95; (pb), $14.95	_____
_____	Recovery From Codependence, (hc) $21.95; (pb) $13.95	_____
_____	Renewed Each Day, 2-Volume Set, (pb) $27.90	_____
_____	Seeking the Path to Life (pb), $14.95	_____
_____	Self, Struggle & Change (hc), $21.95	_____
_____	Shabbat Seder (pb), $14.95	_____
_____	So That Your Values Live On (hc), $23.95; (pb), $16.95	_____
_____	Spirit of Renewal (hc), $22.95; (pb), $16.95	_____
_____	A Time to Mourn (pb), $16.95	_____
_____	Tormented Master (pb), $17.95	_____
_____	Twelve Jewish Steps To Recovery, (hc) $19.95; (pb) $13.95	_____
_____	When a Grandparent Dies (hc), $14.95	_____
_____	Your Word Is Fire (pb), $14.95	_____

• The Kushner Series •

_____	The Book of Letters Popular Hardcover Edition (hc), $24.95	_____
_____	The Book of Words (hc), $21.95	_____
_____	God Was in This Place... (hc) $21.95; (pb) $16.95	_____
_____	Honey from the Rock (pb), $14.95	_____
_____	Invisible Lines of Connection (hc), $21.95	_____
_____	River of Light (pb), $14.95	_____

For s/h, add $3.50 for the first book, $2.00 each add'l book (to a max. of $10.00) $ s/h _____

TOTAL _____

Check enclosed for $_____ *payable to:* JEWISH LIGHTS Publishing
Charge my credit card: ❏ MasterCard   ❏ Visa   ❏ AMEX
Credit Card # _____ Expires _____
Name on card _____
Signature _____ Phone (____) _____
Name _____
Street _____
City / State / Zip _____

Phone, fax, or mail to: JEWISH LIGHTS Publishing
P. O. Box 237, Sunset Farm Offices, Route 4, Woodstock, Vermont 05091
Tel **(802) 457-4000**   *Fax* **(802) 457-4004**
Credit card orders (800) 962-4544 (9AM–5PM ET Monday–Friday)
Generous discounts on quantity orders. SATISFACTION GUARANTEED. Prices subject to change.

**AVAILABLE FROM BETTER BOOKSTORES.
TRY YOUR BOOKSTORE FIRST.**

# of Copies	*Order Information*	$ Amount
_____	Aspects of Rabbinic Theology (pb), $18.95	_____
_____	Bar/Bat Mitzvah Basics (hc), $24.95; (pb), $16.95	_____
_____	Being God's Partner (hc), $19.95	_____
_____	But God Remembered (hc), $16.95	_____
_____	The Earth Is the Lord's (pb), $12.95	_____
_____	The 11th Commandment (hc), $16.95	_____
_____	Embracing the Covenant (pb), $15.95	_____
_____	The Empty Chair (hc), $9.95	_____
_____	Finding Joy (hc), $19.95	_____
_____	God & the Big Bang (hc), $21.95	_____
_____	God's Paintbrush (hc), $16.95	_____
_____	Godwrestling—Round 2 (hc), $23.95	_____
_____	Hanukkah (pb), $14.95	_____
_____	Healing of Soul, Healing of Body (pb), $14.95	_____
_____	How to Be a Perfect Stranger (hc), $24.95	_____
_____	In God's Name (hc), $16.95	_____
_____	The Last Trial (pb), $17.95	_____
_____	Lifecycles, Volume 1 (hc), $24.95	_____
_____	Lifecycles, Volume 2 (hc), $24.95	_____
_____	Mourning & Mitzvah (pb), $19.95	_____
_____	The NEW Jewish Baby Book (pb), $15.95	_____
_____	One Hundred Blessings Every Day, (pb), $14.95	_____
_____	A Passion for Truth (pb), $18.95	_____
_____	Passover Seder (pb), $14.95	_____
_____	Putting God on the Guest List (hc), $21.95; (pb), $14.95	_____
_____	Recovery From Codependence, (hc) $21.95; (pb) $13.95	_____
_____	Renewed Each Day, 2-Volume Set, (pb) $27.90	_____
_____	Seeking the Path to Life (pb) $14.95	_____
_____	Self, Struggle & Change (hc) $21.95	_____
_____	Shabbat Seder (pb), $14.95	_____
_____	So That Your Values Live On (hc), $23.95; (pb), $16.95	_____
_____	Spirit of Renewal (hc), $22.95; (pb), $16.95	_____
_____	A Time to Mourn (pb), $16.95	_____
_____	Tormented Master (pb), $17.95	_____
_____	Twelve Jewish Steps To Recovery, (hc) $19.95; (pb) $13.95	_____
_____	When a Grandparent Dies (hc), $14.95	_____
_____	Your Word Is Fire (pb), $14.95	_____

• *The Kushner Series* •

# of Copies		$ Amount
_____	The Book of Letters Popular Hardcover Edition (hc), $24.95	
_____	The Book of Words (hc), $21.95	_____
_____	God Was in This Place... (hc) $21.95; (pb) $16.95	_____
_____	Honey from the Rock (pb), $14.95	_____
_____	Invisible Lines of Connection (hc) $21.95	_____
_____	River of Light (pb), $14.95	_____

For s/h, add $3.50 for the first book, $2.00 each add'l book (to a max. of $10.00) $ s/h _____

TOTAL _____

Check enclosed for $_____ *payable to:* JEWISH LIGHTS Publishing
Charge my credit card: ❐ MasterCard   ❐ Visa   ❐ AMEX
Credit Card # _____ Expires_____
Name on card_____
Signature_____ Phone (_____)_____
Name_____
Street_____
City / State / Zip_____

Phone, fax, or mail to: **JEWISH LIGHTS Publishing**
P. O. Box 237, Sunset Farm Offices, Route 4, Woodstock, Vermont 05091
Tel (802) 457-4000   *Fax* (802) 457-4004
Credit card orders (800) 962-4544 (9AM–5PM ET Monday–Friday)
Generous discounts on quantity orders. **SATISFACTION GUARANTEED.** *Prices subject to change.*

AVAILABLE FROM BETTER BOOKSTORES.
TRY YOUR BOOKSTORE FIRST.